An American in Acapulco:

Dodging Raindrops and Bullets

An American in Acapulco:

Dodging Raindrops and Bullets

John R. Lyman

FIRST EDITION

"Mexico" by John McCrea
© 1998 Stamen Music BMI admin. by Wixen Music Publishing, Inc.

All Rights Reserved. Used by Permission

ISBN: 978-0-692-55752-5

Contents

Prologue

Acapulco was paradise to me. I fell in love with its tropical wonders the first time I set foot there, as so many had before me. The heat envelopes you and never lets go. Sunshine dominates year round, arriving early and staying late. Acapulcans are warm, albeit wary. The cuisine is simple, but exquisite. The party never stops there. A subtle undertone of sexuality pervades the city. Rural escapes are a short drive away; lagoons, cabañas, palm forests, and hammocks await. Iguanas, cuijas, scorpions, bats, giant cockroaches, tarantulas, wild dogs, cats, and squirrels, all can be found with a sharp eye. Winter never touches Acapulco, *es la ciudad de verano eterno.*

When I moved there in 2007, I moved there to stay. And yet, ten years later, my condo has been sold and I may never return.

Mexican beer commercials of recent years say "find your beach". I *found* my beach. And now it's virtually destroyed and, for me, uninhabitable.

This is why.

Oh, Baby, I was bound,
For Mexico,
Oh, Baby, I was bound,
To let you go

"Mexico"
Cake

Flight

One Thursday morning, January 20th, 2011, as I went about my business at home in Sunny Acapulco, my telephone rang. The call would change my life. The man on the line said he was a Federal Police Officer. He informed me that there had been a report of suspicious activity occurring in my area, the caller had said that there were white SUVs circling the block and the report had come from my phone number. Did I call in such a report? Absolutely not. Could anyone have done so from my phone? Only if they were somehow falsely identifying their phone number as mine. Nevertheless, I was terrified.

The caller said, "we have proof, we know it was from your phone". Then he asked me if I had heard about all the beheadings in the Acapulco area. Of course I knew about them, they were a constant occurrence. He continued, his commander needed proof that I wasn't doing anything to threaten the narcos' activities. He said his commander was willing to accept 25,000 pesos to hand over the tape and forget the whole thing. I told him that I didn't have that much money. He asked me how much money I had with me. I said about 800 pesos. He wanted to know how much I could get today, quickly, urgently. I told him I could probably come up with 10,000 pesos. In order for him to allow me to gather the money he was demanding, I had to explain who I could get the money from, how long it would take, and whether I was sure he would give it to me. Grasping at plausible lies, I thought of my friend Miguel who worked about 15 minutes away in Costa Azul. Have I gotten money from him before?, he asked. No, never. How sure are you he will give it to you? Very sure. How far is it, when will you have the money? It's 11:20 a.m., I could get it by 1:00. If I were to do what I said I would, it would have taken me over an hour, round trip to Costa Azul, and back.

After repeatedly demanding I comply with his requests, and making me wait as he spoke to his "commander" a number of times, he agreed to let me go for the money. He asked me whether Soriana, a large grocery store with a number of locations in Acapulco, or Banamex, a bank which had many branches in the vicinity, was more accessible. I said I preferred Soriana. He communicated with his commander again and they decided Banamex was best. He would give me the details about a bank account into which I had to deposit 10,000 pesos by 1:00 p.m. He seemed to have difficulty getting the account number right, almost as if he were so illiterate that reading a number was a challenge to him, adding to the surrealness of the matter.

He asked me how many cell phones were in my house, and mentioned "just mine and my girlfriend's", as if somehow he knew I had one, or more. It was scary, I felt very vulnerable and I thought they had some way of knowing these things, then again, I didn't have a cell phone, so that was a clue to his lack of credibility. I was naive and frightened. Since he had told me originally that they had a report about my phone, and calls made from it, it wasn't a stretch to think that they knew about any other phones in my house. However I did not have, and had never had, a cell phone in Acapulco, other than one a co-worker had loaned me years earlier when I didn't have a phone at my apartment. It was all very intimidating, strange, scary, and shocking. In spite of obvious discrepancies in his story, I was as frightened as I had ever been in my life.

He informed me that they had someone on my street, mentioned it by name, and again made me feel that he had inside knowledge about me. He finally got through reciting the bank account number that I was to use for the deposit. Then he explained exactly what he wanted me to say at the bank. I was to tell them that I wanted to make a deposit into my personal account and give them the number. He made me write the number down and read it back to him. He also made me write down the exact words I was to use when I spoke to the bank teller.

He asked me if I were Mexican, most likely because of my accent. He said I seemed like a rational, reasonable, non-confrontational guy. I said I was, and that I didn't want any problems with anyone. He insisted repeatedly that I keep the telephone line open, leave my wife there and go, and said that if I didn't do what he instructed me to do, my family and I would be his gang's next victims.

When he finally shut up and allowed me to proceed with his demands, I put down the phone I had been talking on and lifted the receiver on the other extension. I then disconnected the cordless phone, planning to take it with me when I left Acapulco that afternoon. I took the batteries out of it and inadvertently ended the call. All the while I was packing I thought he was on the line. If they were outside watching my apartment and I hung up, I figured they'd come and get me. I was shaking and my thoughts were racing. What to take? Who to call? Should I shower or just flee? I got online and sent my sister Ann, and my friend Joe, emails about what had happened, scared Ann quite a bit, Joe didn't see the gravity in the situation.

I had already packed some stuff, I was planning to move back to Chicago on a part-time basis in June, so my departure now was sudden, but not entirely unexpected. Whether I was legitimately in danger, or not, I wasn't willing to discover by risking my life. The fact that three separate mass killings of 18+ people had occurred in Acapulco recently, and the fact that my best friend and two other friends had been killed, made it easy to believe the worst.

Since these events occurred, I have, more than a few times, said to myself, I wonder what would have happened if I had just feigned lack of knowledge of Spanish. It all probably would have ended immediately. I also could have just hung up. In the days and weeks after the call, many of my friends in Acapulco told me they have gotten similar calls and just hung up. I should have done the same. Hindsight is 20/20.

In my defense, I have to mention, I am not an actor, nor a good liar. For me, it is much harder to act as if I don't speak Spanish, than to speak it, which I have done fluently for more than half my life now. As a teacher of children as well as adults, I know one of the biggest barriers to an adult's learning a second language is his/her fear of looking stupid. We all have egos and we want to show our intelligence, not lack of it. Since I am fluent, I don't pretend not to understand, it is completely unnatural to do that now.

Departure

I was shaking like a leaf. I booked a flight online with Continental because I knew their schedule and it was the first carrier to come to mind. The flight was leaving at about 3 p.m. so I had more than three hours to get to the airport. I showered and began to pack. I took my Tivo, and a bunch of other electronic equipment, and put it all into one of the boxes I had had made for transporting my LPs. I already had my turntable, some clothes, and some booze packed in a suitcase. I was still under the impression that my phone line was occupied by that bastard, so I didn't think I could make calls from my apartment.

My custom made wooden cat carrier had two parts divided by a wire screen. This would allow two cats to travel in it without the danger of attacking each other. I took Hamlet and Chivo and put them into it. I put Squeaky into a pet carrier bag, planning to take him onboard the flight. With difficulty, I carried the bulky wooden cage down to my car. I had to put the convertible top down so I could get it in, and it barely fit in the back seat. When I commissioned the cage some months earlier, I had carefully followed the requirements for pet carriers I found online, in an effort to be certain the box would not be rejected by any airline I chose to fly. I loaded my suitcase into the trunk and put the other custom-made box with the electronic equipment on the front seat. Squeaky fit on the floor in the front seat.

Now it was time for my low speed, O.J. Simpson-like, race to the airport. Was anyone watching me? Would I be stopped and confronted en route to the airport? At the end of my street? I had no idea. I kept one eye on the road and the other on the people and vehicles around me. I drove cautiously, but, (isn't there always a but?), somehow I managed to catch the eye of one of the infamous Mexican transit police.

I was just entering the oceanside drive called "La Escénica". After I had driven about a quarter mile up it, as if on cue, police lights go on and I'm ordered to pull over. This asshole says I not only ran a red light, but that I passed a crosswalk in doing so, resulting in an even bigger violation of traffic code. He gets on his cell phone and supposedly calls a tow truck to come get my car. This is just what I need. I'm running for my life, afraid of every damn cop more than ever, and this guy says he's taking my car, with my cats, until I pay 1,200 pesos. This was the second highest amount the Mexican police had attempted to extort from me in the entire eight years I had been living down there. It was outrageous. Usually they take 20 pesos and let you go on your way. The officer said that since there were two infractions he had no choice but to tow my car.

Driving my Celica in Acapulco meant I had to carry copies of official customs documents at all times to prove it was legally there and I was the owner. He asked to see them. I gave them to him and he said they were not sufficient, that they had to be originals. This was not true, I couldn't always carry my original visa, title, and customs permit in the car. In the previous ten or more times I had been stopped, the copies had always been sufficient. This was another ploy to get more money out of me. Fortuitously, this time, since I was leaving the country,

I had packed them in my suitcase. After some attempts at resolving the issue as one normally would, with a bribe, I finally said that I had the documents with me. I opened my trunk and found them, without too much difficulty, in my suitcase. I was doing whatever I could not to let him see all the valuable stuff I had in the car.

When he asked where I was going I told him I was going to see a friend at a shopping mall on the other side of the mountain. This was a fabrication, but I did have a friend who worked there, so that made the lie easier to come up with. He probably knew I was bullshitting from the fact that my car was loaded with cats and luggage, but he didn't make anything of that.

Finally he graciously agreed to accept 800 pesos, (probably close to two weeks pay for him), to let me go. After he left I made it to the airport without incident, but, strangely enough, the fun was just beginning.

Logic would dictate that I was in the clear once I got to the airport after having my life threatened and a significant amount of money extorted from me as a bribe on the drive over, but such was not the case. Things did get better, but my urgent departure would be delayed by 48 hours and I would go back to my apartment multiple times before leaving Mexico.

From the moment the agents at Continental Airlines saw me with my big wooden cat carrier they said there was no way I was getting on one of their flights with my three cats. I was distraught. I was trying to be as calm as possible but I was still terrified that my life was in danger. My only other option was to find another airline that would work with me. American Airlines saved me and my cats.

I remembered that AA had flights that connected to Chicago when CO turned me away. I went immediately to their counter, which was conveniently located next to the Continental check-in area, and explained my predicament. I told them it was urgent that I get a flight to Chicago immediately. I told them I was traveling with multiple live animals. I even told them that I was in fear for my life. The difference between CO and AA was night and day. American quickly began doing all they could to help me travel that day on their afternoon flight. They got in touch with the captain to see if he would allow one of my cats in the cabin with no advanced notice. They also investigated whether the cats in the carrier would pass air travel requirements for pets.

Within a short time they determined that, due to the temperature in Chicago, which was at or below freezing, no animal could travel in the cargo hold. But these kind souls were not done trying to resolve the matter. They told me they'd let me put two cats in one carrier, another in a second one and I could get on board with all of them by eliciting the help of another passenger who would temporarily claim the second carrier contained his/her pet. The rule is that no passenger can take more than one pet in the cabin. They were letting me take three. I was overwhelmed with gratitude and relief. Things seemed to be falling into place.

After completing check-in, I struggled to carry all my cats up to the second floor security check point. In order to pass through the scanner and not put my cats through the x-ray, I had to take each cat out of his carrier and go through the metal detector with them one at a time. I went through the process three times, plus once by myself. Other than the struggle to get them each out and then back into the bags, it all went well.

I reached the gate and sat down to compose myself before the flight boarded. The departure time came and went. I began to get worried. We waited, and waited, and waited. Eventually we were informed that there was a mechanical issue with the aircraft. There were only a few dozen people waiting to board, it was clearly not a full flight. After more than an hour passed we were informed that the flight was being cancelled. I would have to spend another night in the danger zone that Acapulco had become to me. And I'd have to relive the nightmare of carting my cats from the airport to my apartment and back again.

All of us who had been waiting for the flight shuffled back to the point of check-in and formed a new line, I brought up the rear, being the slowest to get back there. That line was moving at a glacial pace. The American Airlines agents didn't seem to have a sensible plan of action for dealing with 30-40 passengers who needed to be rebooked and/or put up in hotels for the night. The first three passengers hadn't even been dispatched after a full half hour had passed. I was stuck with three scared kitties at the back of the line that appeared would last many hours.

Suddenly my luck took a 180 degree turn and the same guy and girls who had been so helpful in the first place called me up to the front of the line. I happily schlepped my cats and other stuff over and they explained what my options were. I could take a flight the next day that would connect in Dallas, or I could wait two days for a non-stop flight to Chicago. Either way my room and board would be covered by the airline. It was an easy choice, I opted for the two day layover and was rebooked and sent on my way. This meant I could contact people in Acapulco before leaving suddenly without even a goodbye, plus I could park my car at my apartment rather than leave it at the airport indefinitely, at a cost of $20 a day. Moreover, I could leave the cat carrier box at my apartment. This was the best outcome possible in every respect.

I picked up my girlfriend Johana, summoned all my nerve, and went to my apartment to drop off my cats. After getting the cats settled, we went to my vet's office and explained what had happened with the carrier. She was glad to take it off my hands and gave me a nice, brand new, pet carrier-bag in exchange. She definitely got the long end of the stick, but I was happy to find a solution that worked for everyone. The second pet carrier bag I had was in poor shape, so a new one was a blessing. A few months later, she told me that she keeps birds in the carrier now. It's gratifying that it was put to good use, it had cost me about $200.

I couldn't have chosen a better hotel to end up at than the Grand Hotel. I had never known what it was called, although I had passed it dozens of times. It is located at the end of the Costera, right before the Boulevard of the Nations, aka "La Escénica". It was quite empty and pretty bare. It was warm, not cold, though.

I played "Smoke on the Water" more than once that evening, it was uncanny how I had ended up, literally, at the Grand Hotel which was empty, (warm) and bare. A funny coincidence.

The Grand is a five star hotel. The two days I spent there were luxurious and passed without incident. They have a few nice, large swimming pools. Curiously, they did not have free Internet so I was unable to contact my sister to let her know I was okay, without paying an exorbitant fee.

On the day of my departure I was transferred to the airport by a mini-van shuttle service. If the whole situation hadn't begun so inauspiciously, it would've been a kind of dream weekend vacation.

Getting checked-in and on board was a piece of cake this time. The American Airlines employees were equally as accommodating this day as they had been previously, and they were expecting me this time, so all went smoothly. A woman in line was chosen to temporarily adopt one of my cats, carrying the bag he was in onto the aircraft with her. Once we were ready for take off I retrieved him and sat, cramped, but happy, surrounded by my three little boys.

Adjusting

I spent the first four months of my trial stay in Acapulco without really making any new friends. I had met a girl named Austria at a print shop in front of my hotel in August, while on vacation there, and told her I'd be moving to Acapulco. She gave me her cell phone number so I could call her when I went back. I hung out with her a few times after I moved down and gave her an English class or two. That friendship dissolved when she tried to steal my video camera.

Two months in, I had been to a few *convivios*, (get-togethers), with my university co-workers, but had no very solid friendships. Arturo Corona, a Universidad Americana de Acapulco, (UAA), teacher, and I got together a few times. He moved to Zihuatanejo after teaching one or two semesters at UAA and we lost touch. I had a pleasant time covering his English class at a Tourism School as a substitute once.

Every one of my co-workers at the university had at least one other teaching job. No one worked full time at UAA. Many of them taught English as a Foreign Language, (EFL), at the various language schools in town, others taught elementary or high school.

Early in my tenure in Acapulco I met Felipe Rico. He was the person I hung out with the most during 2003. We were introduced by Paco Muñoz at his street-corner taco stand, where I spent many nights carousing with the *banda*.

Felipe is a very smooth talker and a world class mooch, he has the ability to ingratiate himself with just about anyone he meets. He speaks English well, is intelligent, and a friendly guy. He had family who lived in Canada and had lived there himself, which was the reason his English was above average. His house was near my job and my apartment. He drank and smoked pot. Since I had very few friends at the time I was open to developing new friendships and I generally tend to hook up with partiers, so it was an easy fit.

He lived about a block and a half away from the university where I worked. I would go there after classes to party with him, sometimes I'd hang out there on my lunch break, too.

During my two years at the university, I was always given a lunch hour, even if I only had two groups of students, so my work day was broken up with a full hour of lunch and only two or three hours of teaching. It was kind of a waste of time, but I did get to walk around the neighborhood, try different restaurants, and mingle with the locals. I met two women I dated, Inés and Ada Lilia, while walking around at lunch time. I would frequently see my students at the restaurants nearby during the break, too.

At Felipe's house we drank, smoked, played ping pong, and pool. He had an in ground swimming pool that I never saw function. It was generally empty or half full of dirty water. The fact that he usually had a few joints to smoke made his company more pleasant, too, but the quality of the weed was often pretty poor. It was apparent that his family had seen much better times, the parts of their house I saw were in serious disrepair. Either that or they just didn't care to maintain and update their home.

In February of 2003 I had a kind of one-night-stand, but it doesn't count as a one-night-stand because we did not have sex. I met a woman at the bar directly in front of the Crowne Plaza Hotel where I went to hear live music. After enjoying the band and having a fun night together, we ended up at my apartment, at the top of Bora Bora. We slept together, but were not intimate.

The morning after our night together I had to go teach. She wanted me to let her stay in my apartment while I was at work. I wasn't about to let her stay. She didn't beg and plead, but she made it clear she thought it was completely logical and sensible for me to let her stay there while I was gone. Reluctantly she accompanied me out the door when I left for the university. I never saw her again.

There are six main reasons why I chose to live in Acapulco. It's on the ocean, I prefer to live within a few miles of a large body of water. It's very hot and I love hot weather. It averages more than 300 days of sunshine per year and the days are long. We are sunshine deprived in Chicago, by my estimate there are about 500 hours more sunlight per year in Acapulco than there are in Chicago, due to latitudinal positions and weather patterns. Acapulco is relatively centrally located in Mexico, I am passionate about travel and discovering new places, cultures, and foods, so being there afforded me access to nearby cities and states. There were very few Americans living there. I did not want to move to Mexico only to be surrounded by a bunch of ex-pats. Finally, I find Acapulcan women to be very attractive, I had dreams of finding a wife.

I planned to travel throughout Mexico using Acapulco as my home base. Before I began teaching at the university in the middle of January, I went to Guanajuato, Guanajuato to see the mummies, technically, petrified bodies. I took in some of the tourist attractions and made a few friends. I met a group of college kids and spent an evening with them. We went to some bars. Late that night we were walking outside and it was extremely cold. It couldn't have been many degrees above freezing and I had no clothes for the occasion. It was awful. I was shivering and uncomfortable. This was, by far, the coldest night I ever spent in any part of Mexico. I exchanged information with two of the girls I met there and would later visit them in Mexico City where they lived. I specifically avoided one of the city's most renowned tourist attractions, "El Callejón del Beso", The Alley of Kisses. Someday I hope to go there with someone to share it with.

I only knew three Americans who lived in Acapulco. One was a woman people called "Dolly" who worked at the university with me. She had been living in Acapulco for about 27 years. Another was a seemingly legitimate businessman whose restaurant had only two locations, one in downtown Chicago and one in Costa Azul, Acapulco, Mother Hubbard's.

The last guy was named Michael and said he was a general contractor from Hawaii. He was a decent enough guy, but inspired little trust in me. He actually told my friend Miguel that he had committed murder and was in Mexico to escape the law. I hired him twice to do some work for me. The second ended poorly. He installed my kitchen cabinets and did a good job. A few months later I had an issue with my shower and asked him to help. I was preparing to return to Chicago due to extreme lack of funds. He got it into his head that I should let him stay in my apartment rent free while I was gone. When he realized that I had no intention of doing so, he became angry and carried out some bizarre retribution by putting cement into my shower drain, rather than fixing the problem he made it much worse. The last time I saw him he begged forgiveness and said he wanted to pay me for the damage. Ultimately he never gave me a dime.

I am sure plenty of people move to Mexico with no skeletons in their closet, but it was pretty obvious that many people did go south to avoid legal complications, therefore, I often made it a point to mention that I was not escaping the law and had complete freedom to cross back and forth as desired.

I rented my first apartment from a family named Maldonado; Don Pépe, the father, Doña Licha, the mother, and the children, Omar, and Mayra. Many interesting encounters were to ensue between us. Generally they were nice, but they had a dark side that made my life unpleasant and difficult.

During my first 16 months living in Acapulco I went back to Chicago a total of seven times. When I left town I had to get someone to take care of my cats. The easiest choice was someone in the family below me. They had dogs and birds, and Mayra appeared responsible and trustworthy enough to feed and maintain my cats.

It will forever remain a mystery exactly what kind of torture they put my cats through, but I know that they would allow their dogs to go up to where my cats were. They were kittens the whole time I lived there. The family's dogs were large and intimidating. My neighbors next door told me they had seen the dogs up bothering my cats, but the Maldonados denied anything of the kind occurring.

Another reason I know they were untrustworthy is this. They had a phone line that was available for use by their renter, in this case, me. I needed a phone and used it at my own expense. However, my bills were much higher than they should have been and on the detailed statements there were calls that I did not make. I finally devised a plan to determine with certainty whether they were abusing my line. One day just after I left home, I called my own number from a pay phone. The line was busy. It remained busy for some time so I knew it wasn't just a call coming in. They were using my line to connect to the Internet.

When I moved out Don Pépe got angry with me because I had taken down some swinging doors in the kitchen. They were very heavy and were a big obstruction in that small space. I had to get a cop I knew to go up to the property with me to mediate matters before my departure. It was agreed that I would re-hang the doors and we would part amicably. Felipe Rico's dad was kind enough to help me replace the doors. It was infinitely easier to take them down than it was to put them back up. None of these things made my stay there comfortable.

Years later I would inadvertently spend a few Sunday afternoons drinking on the beach with the man. By that time he seemed to have no recollection of our unpleasant interactions and just saw us as friends. I wasn't going to hold a grudge, but friends we'll never be.

During my first few years in Acapulco, when George W. Bush was president. When asked, I always felt it was important to tell people that I was American but did not support the U.S. Government's policies. I also explained that I was a certified teacher and not a random American who decided to try to teach English because he spoke it. Moreover, I often had to explain that I was not an outlaw evading capture in the United States. Those were often the types of Americans who moved down there.

One day, shortly after the second Iraq war began, I found myself on the beach with Felipe and we saw a local news network's camera crew filming a shoreline parasail operation. They told us that the parachutes they were using were locally made and emblazoned with the message "No War" in huge letters. Because Felipe was friends with the owners of the operation, he was asked to go up and be filmed while being held afloat by one of the special 'chutes. When he came down he was interviewed briefly by the film crew. After some finagling and paying a nominal price, I was taken up to parasail as well. Upon landing I was also interviewed. They asked me what I thought of Bush and the war. I said the same thing I had been saying for years prior to that. I told them I thought George W. Bush was the devil and I was strongly opposed to this unnecessary war.

The next day I tried to watch the local news to see if I was on it. I went to Felipe's house on my lunch break but his TV was barely working and it was difficult to watch the channel the broadcast was to be on. I will never know if they showed the part where I spoke.

Felipe Rico and Dad

Paco Muñoz

Paco Muñoz was my first real friend in Acapulco. He was a DJ on a local radio station who had a taco cart that was parked near the bottom of the mountain near the street where I lived. Just about every time I came home from work he would speak to me, often in English, trying to get me to try his tacos. I was not particularly inclined to eat there because none of those carts appeared to be very sanitary, but I eventually did and, over time, was eating there pretty much every day while I hung out with him and Chango.

Paco's English is very good. He's a smart, outgoing, friendly person and it was nice to have someone to talk to and hang with. More than anyone else, he was instrumental in my decision to stay in Acapulco permanently.

Paco often invited me to go to the radio station where he was a DJ. One evening I finally did. I spoke Spanish, and some English, on the air, selected some songs, and had a cool experience. The station's limited repertoire and genres didn't leave much room for playing songs I liked, as they played English language pop music, nevertheless, it was lots of fun.

Chango, Carlos, Paco, and Me

Chango and Jaime

Chango, (actual name José), was his cook, a very sweet guy who I never saw argue or get angry. We hung out a few times without the other guys, who all did cocaine. I always abstained from it and Chango only used it rarely. He ended up working for another friend I made through Paco, Carlos Varela. Chango and I often commiserated about our friends' excessive drug use.

One time I ran into a stupid guy, Roberto, who I often saw up at Carlos' dad's restaurant. He told me Chango was dead. I was very relieved when I found out it was just an ignorant joke. It was always hard to stay in touch with Chango because he had no home phone. I haven't heard from him for years now.

About three years after I met Paco he moved to Huatulco, Oaxaca to work at a friend's jewelry store. They specialized in Mexican gold and silver jewelry. His strength is sales and there was a lot of money to be made selling to tourists down there. English speakers are in demand in Huatulco, it is a growing tourist destination and travelers love to buy Mexican gold and silver.

Once I went down to visit him. While I was there we spent very little time together. Either he was heavily using cocaine or he was involved with his boss, the woman who owned the jewelry store, probably both. I went to a party at her house one day before I left. While attempting to make the best of the time I had by myself, I met Noemi, with whom I maintained contact for a few years. She worked at a little place that had about a dozen public telephones, mostly for making long distance calls. Internet cafés and Skype weren't on the scene then.

Noemi came to Acapulco once and we spent the day together. One day out of the blue she called me and said she was in town, it was an awkward morning and afternoon, with little conversation, time moved like molasses. I haven't had contact with her for a few years now. She was from a very small village in Oaxaca and we had little in common.

Jaime Virto was a friend, a DJ, who Paco introduced me to. He was a very large fellow. He used to DJ at a restaurant/bar called Paradise and when he was working we'd buy beers and sneak them in and drink them while the party went on around us. Paradise had a large bar and dance area, all constructed of wood, extending the street and sidewalk closer to the beach. It was almost on top of the water. First he worked upstairs, outdoors, later they moved him downstairs into the DJ booth that serviced the dining room. It was easier to drink and party there, but the booth was very small and Jaime kept it cold with the AC on high. After a few years there Jaime got a new gig next door at Barba Roja, a similar restaurant/bar, and we partied in their DJ booth too.

Jaime, Paco, and Carlos did cocaine often, all except Chango who learned quickly to not indulge, possibly for lack of funds. I think Jaime moved to Cabo so he could keep doing coke in a safer environment, or get away from his contacts in Acapulco. We kept in touch and when he came back to Acapulco once we went to Zydeco together with my girlfriend and his, but now we've lost touch.

Jaime, Paco, and una amiga

Carlos Varela and "El Campanario II"

I considered Carlos Varela my best friend in Acapulco for years. He never asked me for money, he didn't ask me for anything other than friendship. We had similar tastes in music and he liked to hear new stuff I played for him. I made him into a Counting Crows fan and I gave him many CDs and DVDs of their music and concerts. He loved U2 like I did, so I grew his U2 collection by dozens of hours, also.

Our relationship was strained for years by his incessant cocaine use. Time after time I would invite him to go out, or to come to my condo and, time after time, he would say yes and never arrive. Months passed when we would not hang out together, even though we spoke in the evening and agreed to hang out after Carlos got off work. I eventually gave him the nickname "El granjero", (the farmer), because in Spanish when someone stands you up they say "me dejó plantado", (he/she left me planted), since he always left me planted, he was a farmer. It was cocaine every time. I was naive about his heavy habit. Eventually I caught on. His father was even more oblivious than me.

Carlos' father, Don Carmelo, has a successful restaurant in the Alta Progreso housing complex, a steak and seafood restaurant, mostly American style cuisine. Everyone at the restaurant always treated me very well, but Don Carmelo has some weird approaches to life, and people, and he and Carlos fought like lovers. They would break up and reunite over and over. I got quite tired of that.

Carlos's mom had a restaurant too, basically a mirror image of the one his dad had, about half a block down the mountain. So, when Carlos would fight with his dad, he'd go down and work with his mom. He made less money with his mom because the restaurant was smaller and focused on carry out more than dining in. They had eight or ten tables, as compared to 20 at his father's place. The general atmosphere was more relaxed and less elegant than at his dad's restaurant.

Don Carmelo's place had a wonderful view of the bay and had been in existence for over ten years when I got there. They had a devastating fire some years back, but rebuilt and were even more successful afterwards. Some 15 years previously, Don Carmelo had worked at Barba Negra, a high class restaurant on the Costera in the Condesa area. About the time they closed Carmelo opened his own place. He is a very, very hard working man and deserves all his success and prosperity. He never took a day off, and the restaurant was open every day of the year.

He took a perverse pride in saying that "El Barbie" was a client of his. Other narcos may have frequented his place, too. I was ignorant to the nefarious people around me.

One day in 2010, they were robbed at gunpoint, no one was injured, though.

The first victim of the drug war who I knew personally was a waiter at Don Carmelo's restaurant, Geronimo, aka "El Güero". He got involved with selling drugs. His sister Griselda, who had an incredibly sexy body, also worked at the restaurant. They both hung out on my terrace a few times with Carlos and me.

One night, technically, early one morning, I was with Carlos and we were driving around drinking and smoking some bud. We drove across the mountain, on the Boulevard of the Nations, aka "La Escénica" all the way over to the airport. It was about an hour round trip. After we were back on our side of the mountain, we stopped at the 24 hour Walmart to do some late night shopping and to pick up some more booze. When we came out we were loading groceries into my trunk when we were approached by a police patrol car. The officers got out and asked us what we were doing. At that point we were both somewhat toasted and the possibility of being arrested for being under the influence, or for marijuana possession, or both, was a significant concern.

The cops looked in the trunk and saw the groceries. They asked us if we were doing any cocaine or other hard drugs. When they were satisfied that we were not, one of them said that since we were *solo cheleando*, just drinking beers, there was no problem and we were free to continue on our way. It was amusing to me that they didn't care if we were drinking and driving with open beers, but if we were doing something else we would've been run in.

Another night we were driving around, minding our own business, when we got pulled over for no particular reason. As usual, the officers asked to see the importation documents for my car. This time I had an actual, albeit minor, infraction.

My car was initially granted a six-month circulation permit. I was required to register it with Customs once a year at the Port Authority. I had to complete an official letter about my intentions, and also give them a copy of my car title. It was not complicated. There was never any question of whether it would be granted, it was only a matter of filing the paperwork.

This night I was out with Carlos and some other folks and we got pulled over. When I showed them my docs it turned out that I had let the Customs letter expire. They were going to impound my car. We were required to follow the patrol to the station to get it all sorted out. It turned out that someone who was with us was an acquaintance of one of the cops. I know that things would have gone much worse for me if I had been alone. Having an Acapulcan with me certainly saved me money and headaches. As we sat in the station, Carlos and the others discussed the matter with the police. One policeman was acting as good cop and another, not so much. We were negotiating the *mochada*, bribe, that we'd have to pay to let the matter drop. The cops always try to make it seem that you are paying some sort of official fees. I ended up giving them 200 pesos, about $20.

Another time I was out with Carlos and we were walking along near a karaoke bar called Beverly Hills. Carlos had an open Corona with him and the police stopped us. While there are a number of locations around Acapulco where you can drink in public, this was not one of them. As always, I was scared when confronted by what were certainly corrupt cops. I had pot on me, so I was worried they'd search me and we'd be in even deeper shit. They wanted 100 pesos, which is at least five times the typical payoff they normally demand. Carlos wanted to argue and get it reduced. I wanted to get out of there ASAP. I gave them the money and we were on our way, frightened and poorer, but otherwise unharmed.

2,000 Mile Drive

Beautiful Celica

I spent the summer of 2003 in Chicago but had to get back to Acapulco to start the Fall semester. A three day driving trip alone was a scary proposition. My six-month trial move was done via airplane, but to make the permanent move I would have to drive my car down and take my cat Hamlet, as well as some essential belongings. I wasn't going to buy a new car when I had such a nice one already.

While in the Windy City, I met a woman named Maria at the Fireside Restaurant. We dated for a few weeks but that part of the relationship quickly fizzled out. I was nearly desperate for someone to make the 2,200 mile drive with me and she claimed she was born in Acapulco, so she had a special incentive for going. She had not been back there since she was a toddler and was enthusiastic about checking it out.

Maria turned out to be useless on the drive, she slept a lot so she wasn't talking to me to keep me awake, as we had agreed she would. I didn't want to let her drive and she never did. She paid almost nothing and cost us a lot of extra time during the drive south.

Our departure was scheduled for early in the morning. When I picked her up she informed me that she had left her dog at a kennel and had to go there to take care of part of the bill before we left. It was in Northbrook, north of Chicago. She was ready at nine a.m. but the drive to the kennel cost us more than an hour. When I picked her up she had her belongings in a large plastic garbage bag, a brown paper bag, and a small suitcase. She was a mess.

Since my navigational skills are weak and she said hers were strong, I conceded that she should be our navigator. This was a huge mistake. She convinced me to go through Brownsville, Texas where she had friends. Going to Mexico through Brownsville may be shorter as the crow flies, but it is not logical when considering the existing roads, especially the highways, in Mexico.

We stopped somewhere in Arkansas the first night. The second day we reached Brownsville. In spite of my insistence that she be ready to get back on the road by early morning, she stayed out until three a.m. at a strip club, drinking and debauching, and was not ready to leave until the next afternoon. When we finally got on the road we made it to Northern Mexico, passed an uneventful border crossing, and were driving back roads in a rural area surrounded by flora and farms.

All of a sudden, out of nowhere a police car appeared, turned on its lights, and told us to stop. We were in the middle of a corn field. This did not bode well. We stopped, surrounded by nothing more than farmland. My car was completely loaded with stuff. The trunk was full to the brim, principally with stereo equipment, wires, and clothing. The back seat had my cat Hamlet in his carrier, an ice chest, and a ton of other stuff. The cops suspected that we had drugs in the vehicle. I was glad we didn't. I was less concerned about the situation because I knew, no matter how hard, or where they searched, they wouldn't find anything, there was nothing to find. I had deliberately thrown my pipe and a small amount of bud in a garbage can at a gas station just before crossing the border. When we crossed the border with no search I regretted throwing it away, but now I saw that it was for the best. I was oblivious to the reality of how bad this situation could have been. I was confident in my lack of culpability.

The cops emptied the car's trunk onto the road. They searched the interior of the car and found nothing. They were still not satisfied. They decided to remove the mud guards on the floor, along the interior of the doors, thinking something was stashed in the area where the door met the floor. I think my naiveté worked to my advantage. I wasn't nearly as worried then as I would be if that happened today. Finally they decided we were clean and let us proceed on our way. They didn't even take any money from me.

It was getting dark and we had to find a place to spend the night. Unlit country roads at night in Mexico are not only scary but also a challenge to navigate, they are dangerous for a multitude of reasons. An hour after it got dark we found a hotel that had a gated parking lot, which was a relief to me. I snuck Hamlet in and we passed the night without further incident.

Soon after arriving in Acapulco I introduced Felipe and Maria. They were an awful combination of moochers. I rapidly got tired of paying for everything we did. I remember being at a gas station with them, in my car, having little or no money and not getting any cooperation for gas from either of them. The way they leeched everything they could got old very quickly.

I had good times hanging with Felipe, but our friendship ended when some incredibly stupid, bullshit stuff happened between us. His girlfriend Monica and her cousin gossiped about me to him. The cousin, Neivi, was very briefly a student of mine at the university, attending a conversation group I had. I knew her and her clique. For some unfathomable reason this girl, Neivi, decided to tell Felipe I was hitting on Monica. It was a complete fabrication with no basis in fact. I have no idea why she said it. I had to somehow try to prove a negative, that there was nothing going on, so whatever friendship Felipe and I had, and it was never that great, was pushed to near the breaking point. Between his incessant leeching, use of coke in spite of having no money, and the gossip, there were many reasons not to hang out with Felipe Rico. I never spoke with him for the last five years I lived there.

During the first few days after we arrived in Acapulco, Maria stayed with me in my apartment. There was only one bed, so we shared it. It was a sad excuse for a bed, to be blunt, it was a mattress on a frame. The mattress was of the poorest quality and would tip one way or the other if all the weight was on one side. It wasn't hard to get nearly tipped over onto the floor. I ended up sleeping on the floor more than once. If we had been a couple the bed would've been more tolerable, but nothing was further from my mind, I didn't even like her as a friend by then.

We never had agreed specifically where she was supposed to end up staying, I understood she was going to stay with me for the first few days and then find a hotel, or go back to Chicago. She never verbalized a definite time frame for her visit. It didn't take more than three days before I got fed up with financing her activities and sharing my apartment with a worthless lump. During the day when I was at the university she would do nothing. She wouldn't even buy urgently needed toilet paper. She was useless, I got angry and we fought. Within hours after the argument she spoke to my landlord, Señora Sylvia, and lied to her and told her I had kicked her out. The thought had never crossed my mind. The next thing I knew *I* was being told to leave, that the living arrangement wasn't working out. I was dumbfounded. I decided to stay as long as I could because I had nowhere else to go, if Señora Sylvia confronted me again, I'd have to get out.

A day or two after I was told to leave, I saw Maria coming in and out of a room in a different part of the house, down by the garage. It seemed that she would be staying there and I would be leaving. Silvia and I never exchanged any more words on the subject in the immediate days following the misunderstanding. I just wanted to stay, in peace, at the apartment I had contracted to rent before I went to Chicago for the summer. I had never even *considered* making Maria leave. It astonished me that someone could be so low as to make up stories with such serious consequences, especially about someone who helped her as much as I did. The last time I saw her she was walking on Bora Bora Street, the main artery to our street. I have no idea how long she stayed in Acapulco.

On a similar but unrelated note, there was something crazy about the set up at Señora Sylvia's house, besides the fact that I had to walk through their living room to get to my apartment. When I wanted to use my air conditioner I had to risk my life. In the verbal rental agreement we made, it was stipulated that I had air conditioning in my apartment, but only at night and only when I hooked it up illegally.

There was a window unit in my bedroom with an electrical cord running out of it and over the terrace to where the power lines were. Each time I wanted to use the air conditioner I had to go out and place wires, that ran across the terrace 30 feet, over the live power line located about four feet from the terrace railing, risking electrocution from high voltage. Since I love hot weather I didn't do it very often, but there were days when it was impossible to do without, there was almost no air circulation in that space. I did it no more than a dozen times over the year that I lived there. Señora Sylvia admonished me not to do it during the day because if electric company employees saw it, it would cause her and her husband Humberto trouble. It was common practice in Acapulco and many other parts of Mexico to steal electricity and/or alter one's meter.

Club Med

Mexico is rife with bribery as any citizen and many visitors can tell you. Sometimes not paying bribes is a bigger mistake than to settle things with some cash. If you don't do things that way, you will never get results. I paid over a dozen bribes during the time I was in Mexico, always with the goal of escaping a difficult, if not dangerous, situation. Sometimes people use bribes to gain favorable treatment. Teachers are notorious for accepting payoffs, and other favors, for grades.

During my tenure as a teacher, at any level, I was always accessible and had a good rapport with nearly all of my students. At the Universidad Americana de Acapulco I had a student in one of my semi-advanced classes named David Ortiz.

One day I was walking by the shopping center, the Gran Plaza, two blocks from the university. I ran into David and his mom. I had a good relationship with David, I would say he liked me as a professor, so, when I ran into them, he introduced me to his mother. She told me she was in charge of public relations at the Club Med in Ixtapa, naturally I was intrigued. I certainly didn't suggest anything but, without being asked, she said she could get me a weekend there gratis. I have never been a brown-nose, I don't believe in that and I don't accept or encourage anyone to treat me that way. It's easy to believe that she did it to give her son an advantage in my class. Probably a lot of professors in Mexico would give him preferential treatment for something like that. Maybe I was accepting a gift intended to curry favor, but I don't work that way and I didn't alter David's grade in the least way after this. Ultimately, I ended up at the Club Med in Ixtapa for a weekend.

I took a bus from Acapulco for $15, one way, to Zihuatanejo, a kind of a sister city to Ixtapa. Ixtapa is an expensive resort city, Zihuatanejo is more of a normal Mexican seaside town, about fifteen minutes away. Ixtapa is similar to Cancun, it is a tourist based town that grew out of the express desire to create a tourist destination near Zihuatanejo. From there to Ixtapa I had to take a taxi which cost nearly as much as the bus ride all the way from Acapulco. I had been to Zihuatanejo a few times previously, but had never gone to Ixtapa while there.

When I arrived I checked-in and went to see the layout of the resort. I went to the pool and to the beach, I met some folks, mostly younger than me. The staff was largely composed of young guys and alluring girls.

Two memorable things happened that weekend. Saturday, at my first breakfast, I was seated at a large, round table with a Canadian woman, her young-adult daughter, and a couple from the United States. It was Fall of 2003, the U.S. had recently gotten more aggressive in Iraq and the war there was in the news and on our minds. Somewhat naturally, the conversation touched on the war.

At that point in time, the majority of Americans were in favor of W's invasion of Iraq. When the subject came up I was enthusiastically willing to share my opinion. I said that I was completely against the invasion, I felt the Iraqis were no threat to the United States, and that they had no long range missile capabilities, nor the infamous WMD. Besides, they were not responsible for 9/11. I saw it as a war being fought because Bush wanted a war. My Mexican friends all said it was because of oil. At the time I disagreed, but now it is clear they were right.

The American couple wasn't having any of what I was puttin' down. They got up and left while I was back at the buffet. I deeply offended them unintentionally. Since I still feel strongly that the whole thing was a debacle, and over one thousand Americans lost their lives there, while many more were wounded, I won't apologize for being outspoken about what I think.

Another Club Med highlight was the woman I met Saturday night. Multiple bars were found around the complex where a variety of activities were offered for guests. We met over some drinks at one of these spots. She was more than ten years older than me. She and I talked and flirted over the course of the evening and I ended up going back to her room. I rarely find myself in bed with a woman the night I meet her, but this was one of those times. The environment was ideal for a hook-up and I was up for one.

Although we ended up in bed, things never got as passionate as I had hoped. She was resisting and my motto was, is, and always will be, "if they resist, don't insist". Gentlemen do exist and I'm one of them. Sex would've been a natural conclusion to the evening. It was not meant to be. No problem, probably for the best.

Utility Hook Ups and Squirrels

In Mexico, when you buy a condominium, especially a new construction, you get very few of the features Americans expect in a house or condominium. There are no light fixtures, no closets, no kitchen cabinets, no appliances and, in my case, no electricity connection, no telephone, and no gas. The contractor who built the edifice assured me that my condominium would have properly connected electricity, but he was not a man of his word. After weeks of unfulfilled promises, I knew I would have to get the connection myself.

My apartment is not easy to find, even the most Acapulcan Acapulcan doesn't know where it is. It's very easy to drive by the street because it is small and looks like a driveway more than a street. Locating it for the first time is a challenge. When it comes to getting service people to arrive there, it is no small task. This made obtaining a legal light connection even more difficult.

From the day I moved in I had an illegal electricity hookup and didn't want it that way. The construction workers who built the condominium had rigged things so they had electricity and that connection was what I relied on. I asked some friends, Juan and Jesus, who worked for the Commission, the Mexican electric company, to set me up correctly. They were very willing to promise to help me, but never did help in any way.

The bulk of the grunt work to get me connected was done by Carlos Varela's brother-in-law, Luis. He worked for the Commission as some kind of technician, I paid him 2,000 pesos, about $200. He went up a pole on a wall outside my house and connected the main wires, but it still wasn't a legal connection. The wiring was done, but I still had to get other Commission employees to come and install a meter.

One of the men who installed the meter advised me that the fuse box / breaker that connected to the outside line was not up to code and that the panel had to have a cage around it due to the amount of voltage it conducted. This was undoubtedly a con to get some cash. He told me there were multiple infractions, but once the meters were installed the alleged problems vanished, I became a proper electricity customer with a proper bill. I finally had a legal connection.

A handyman who did some work for me once told me that my whole apartment was not correctly grounded, but over the years I had less problems with electric equipment going bad there than I had had at my other two apartments, so I think he was wrong. However, I always used the highest quality surge protectors I could find, imported from the USA.

Looking back, the electric service in Acapulco was quite good. It did go out on occasion, and I remember hearing, more than once, in the vicinity, explosions that sounded like transformers blowing up, then the power would go out, but it didn't usually stay off too long.

Many locals have altered electric meters that run slower than the actual level of use, but my electric bill was never so high that I had a need, or desire, to rig mine like that.

Soon after moving into the condo, I put up a lightweight gazebo on the roof for my English classes. The sun was brutally scorching during the day and the days lasted 12 hours or more. The plastic tubes designed to hold the thing together could not withstand the strong winds that blew on my terrace. I had Daniel, "El Diablo", a handyman Carlos Varela had introduced me to, try to swap the original tubes with metal pipes, hoping that they would make it strong enough to withstand the winds. It was not an easy task to get the thing reconstructed that way.

In my typical naiveté, before he completed the job, I gave Daniel more money than I owed him, expecting him to come back to finish everything. He never did. My efforts to recuperate the funds were futile, he ducked my calls and lied to me for some weeks, until I finally gave up and wrote off the cash. I eventually realized that a gazebo was not enough and I had a concrete roof put in, over about 40% of the terrace.

My future girlfriend, Johana, lived two doors down from "El Diablo". He and his family had frequent disagreements with the neighbors, including Johana's family. Once someone tried to burn his house down, rumored to be the result of a serious disagreement. The family was displaced for a while after the fire, either because of damage, fear, or both.

His front yard, which was actually two parking spaces, was a huge pile of junk, Fred Sanford style. He had a number of broken down cars that took up more spaces, too. That parking area was bad enough without him commandeering four, or more, spots. This section of the apartment complex was on a steep incline and dead ended at the top, where Johana lived. On nights when I dropped her off late, she would get out and direct me as I maneuvered, inches from the cars in front and back of me, while making a u-turn. It was a relief every time there was an open parking space I could back into while turning around.

Getting properly connected to the water main was also a long, drawn-out challenge. In Mexico, you don't just connect to the main water line, at least not in a new building in a somewhat secluded location in Acapulco.

Our building was built without a proper connection to the main line and sewer. It had a septic tank that had no connection to the sewer or other plumbing. By law you are required to be connected to the city line, but through whatever means, the builder was given permission to build with only an input, not an output.

Under the building we had the septic tank and a back up tank of water. The reserve tank lacked a pump to get its water up to the tanks on the roof and we never did get it hooked up, in spite of running out of water many times. The septic tank had to be emptied occasionally, but over time my neighbor, Dolores, stopped telling me it needed to be done, most likely just paying for that herself.

There was some urgency to getting the building connected properly so we would not need the septic tank. If a building made of concrete and iron is exposed to human waste, over time it will deteriorate dangerously. Dolores said we needed to get connected to the city sewer because of the corrosive quality of wastewater that sat in the septic tank under our building. She worked continuously from the time she moved in to get us connected, and she finally succeeded while simultaneously getting the street paved. Then she had to leave because she couldn't pay her mortgage.

In Mexico they say that whatever happens in the U.S. has direct consequences on their economy, "*si Estados Unidos estornuda, se enferma México*", if the United States sneezes, Mexico gets sick. There have certainly been far too many people who lost their homes up north, she can be included in the tally down south. She was a perfect balance to the awful, argumentative, uncooperative family who lived on the second floor and I missed her immensely after she left.

It's possible that I could have lived without official water service at my condo for years without a water meter, but I don't operate like that, I wanted my services legally delivered and paid for. My friend Miguel Acevedo helped me get connected through an introduction to his friend Felipe.

One day Miguel invited me to a city called Hacienda de Cabañas, in the direction of Zihuatanejo, about two hours north of Acapulco. We agreed to meet at a mall on Calzada Pie de la Cuesta, a road that leads out of Acapulco. There was a grocery store there, where I could park my car for free all day and we could drive together to the town. Besides Miguel, his wife Adelina, his two daughters, his son, and me, other friends of his went; El Medico, El Tocayo and a guy named Felipe. There were nine of us, we went in two cars.

We spent the day drinking, playing Frisbee, eating, chatting, and hanging out. I spoke about my difficulties getting a water connection and Felipe told me he'd get me hooked up. Later that week I went to his office near *El Zocalo*, gave him three or four thousand pesos, and he began taking steps to get me connected to the main line.

Within a short period of time representatives of the water commission came to begin the process. I learned that when you get connected like that in a new building in Acapulco you have to buy all the parts, valves, copper pipes, sandpaper, glue, all the stuff necessary to complete the connection.

The first day they arrived and assessed what would need to be purchased for the work to be done. I made a list. The hardware store where I got the supplies had a weird setup where the product was behind a partition. Customers would tell an employee what they needed and he/she would go find it and bring it back. One group of employees would find your items and make an invoice. Then you'd get in another line and pay your bill. Theft by customers was virtually eliminated.

Once I was connected, everything's cool, right? No such luck. I didn't have a meter, I couldn't get officially connected without a meter. All they had done was make the pipe from the main line reach my building, but they did not actually connect me. I gave Felipe another thousand pesos, we went to a CAPAMA office, (water commission), and he gave the money to someone there. Subsequent events gave me the impression that the money, and the person he gave it to, never helped me in any way. I was told there were no water meters available in Acapulco and would have to wait until some more arrived. After more weeks waiting, the men arrived and installed the meter and it was done.

Part of the urgency for getting a water account of my own was my neighbors and the fact that we all shared a common water bill. There were four people on the second floor, a mother, her two daughters, and son. The woman on the first floor lived with her son and mother, so there were eight people using the water and each had access to the same, limited supply. The cost was divided in three parts, so I was paying 33% of the bill and using about 13% of the water. Moreover, on more than one occasion we ran out of water completely, so if I had my own supply I might avoid running out of water when it was more scarce. It was imperative that I get my own account. As the years passed it would become evident that having my own tank was not only a benefit, but also a liability.

One day, in an attempt to resolve our struggle to get our building connected to the sewer system, I went to an official meeting at the Water Commission with my neighbor, Dolores. We were among other residents of Guerrero, some very humble folks, who were pleading for the city to connect them to the water main. They had travelled a long distance to demand help because they were living without any real water supply, other than tanker trucks that delivered water on a sporadic basis, at a cost far higher than what regular water consumers paid. These humble souls had lived that way for many years and were at the end of their rope. At the conclusion of the meeting nothing had been resolved for us and the other folks were still pleading their case.

Getting a phone line wasn't as problematic, but after I got one, I had a problem with squirrels chewing the wire for years. Many phone calls to Telmex resulted in the situation being investigated. At least five different technicians came to my place over the period I had these difficulties. Whenever it rained my Internet and phone would go out. Even on clear days the connection was poor and none of the guys who arrived to check it ever determined what was going on. My phone would disconnect calls all the time and the sound was dismal. I continued to pester them until they got sick enough of me to send someone capable of discerning the problem. He figured it out.

Direct TV and a Giant Dish

It took me some time to figure out that the only way I would be able to watch American TV programs, and the Chicago Cubs, would be to get a Direct TV account from the United States. I had spoken a few times to the manager of Referees where they had multiple American satellite signals on their televisions. He told me all I needed was a large satellite dish and I could get a pirated Direct TV card from him. I chose not to do it quite so illegally.

I found a very basic Direct TV box at ABT Electronics for $60.00 with no strings attached, no contract required. It was the perfect option for me. I contracted service with the understanding that I would do a self-install. Then I took the box to Acapulco and investigated how to get a six foot satellite dish installed on my roof.

The guy at Referee's put me in touch with an employee of Sky Satellite TV. I thought he must be moonlighting and that his employer would not be happy if he found out what he was doing. Nothing ever proved this to be true. After a few weeks he located a giant dish. It cost about $600 installed.

Although my roof is over four stories above the ground, these guys were professionals and they got it up and installed without incident. It turned out to be much easier to contract an illegal satellite TV connection than it was to get a legitimate water, electric, or telephone account.

Over time I learned that heavy rain and clouds would block my TV signal, so during storms my signal would go out. I'm not sure whether that happens as much in the United States, maybe it's the same everywhere, but I thought it might be related to my distance from where the signal was supposed to be reaching and where it actually was being received.

Although the connection worked, it did not receive the free, network channels that any television in the U.S. gets. These are the channels that have many of the shows I like. I could get WGN America which broadcast the Cubs games when they weren't on CSN, a basic cable channel. I tried to find out how I could get those channels, because they are broadcast like other typical cable channels to places where they are inaccessible through normal over-the-air reception, like remote mountain areas. In the end I was unable to do anything but accept the fact that I couldn't get those channels. I asked the owner of Mother Hubbard's, a Chicagoan, who also had a satellite dish set up like I did, if he got all those channels. He claimed he did, but I doubt that was true. As I got to know him more I found he was a real curmudgeon, further weakening his credibility.

My father was kind enough to record the two shows I cared most about, "Survivor" and "The Amazing Race". After he died, I found out about a device called "Slingbox" which allowed me to send a TV/Tivo signal through the Internet. The signal was much lower quality than through Direct TV, but I had access to all programming.

It was a challenge to get the Direct TV signal activated, or, after service issues, restored. The only phone number they offered for customer service was a toll free 800 number and those were difficult, if not impossible, to call from

Mexico. One time I had my dad do a three-way call so I could speak to them and get the connection functioning. Eventually, I got a phone card that did allow me to call those numbers and then, finally, I got a Skype account and phone, which allowed me to call any number I wanted.

As the years passed Direct TV came out with new options like HD, dual tuners and DVR/cable box combinations. I examined the connectors on my satellite dish and saw that there was a dual plug. I was psyched to think that all I needed was a new dual tuner box and I could receive and record two shows at once. When I put it to the test I learned that I was seriously mistaken.

I repeated the steps I had previously taken. I went to ABT and found a dual tuner/DVR Direct TV box. It was nearly $300, five times the price of the other one, but apparently worth the expense.

Upon return to Acapulco I ran a second cable from the dish to the box. There was no second signal. I called Direct TV and tiptoed around the fact that I wasn't in the United States. They did everything they could on their end, but to no avail.

I went to the Sky office and spoke to the guy who had installed my dish in the first place. He informed me that only by having two dishes could I watch two programs simultaneously. That was not going to happen.

It was difficult to interchange the dual tuner box with the old one. I was afraid Direct TV was getting suspicious and they had rules about how often you could change your account. Service for the HD/DVR box was significantly more costly than it was for the old, basic box, so I did save money by not installing the new one, but it took time to get it all back the way it had been.

Over a period of a few months I had to keep stalling Direct TV about returning the access card that went with the new box, I was not going to return to Chicago anytime soon. They were threatening to charge me steep penalties. When I finally got back there and sent it to them they had another surprise for me. The box that I had bought, I hadn't technically bought. It was some kind of lease and I had to return it or pay hundreds of dollars. No one had told me anything of the kind when I bought it. For another few months I had to stall Direct TV further before I could get the box and return it to them. I had left it in Mexico. It was very strange to buy a component for $300.00 and then be told I did not own it.

Me and the Big Dish

Terrace Roof and Bathroom

Spiral Staircase to Terrace

Rosa Virgen

On December 31st, 2002, days after my Acapulco adventure began, my friends Karla, Hector, their son Erick, and I went to the Sam's Club near my apartment, we were shopping for the ingredients for a special New Year's Eve feast. Within minutes of entering the store I was greeted by a pretty, smiling face, Rosa Virgen Olea, (Rosy), who would become a good friend. She was offering samples of cheese to customers, doing promotion. We hit it off immediately and she invited me to her house for dinner that night. I was reluctant to say yes, I was trepidatious about how I would make it to her house with no car and no real knowledge of the geography of Acapulco, at night, on New Year's Eve. Plus I didn't want to commit to dinner when would be eating at my place.

Karla, Hector, Erick and I made a bunch of dishes, drank a bit, and enjoyed a New Year's Eve meal on my terrace, technically the roof of my apartment, with a distant view of the bay.

At about 9:00 p.m. Rosy called me and gave me information about where to meet her. I struggled to be certain of the name of the neighborhood she gave me, *La Garita*, we would meet at a church there. It was located up the mountain about a half a mile, a ten minute walk away, but I did not know that at the time. Her family lived in a neighborhood on the other side of the mountain called *La Sabana*, which faces inland and does not have a view of the sea. When I got to the church I picked up Rosy and we continued in my taxi to her house. The taxi dropped us off on a main street and from there we walked up some winding, unpaved, uneven, mountain roads to her house. Their home was humble, but nice, and her family was very friendly to me. I developed a friendship with them all.

In spite of my attempts to politely decline their food, they talked me into eating some. I did not want to be rude, however crammed my stomach was already. That was the first time I had tried homemade tamales wrapped in banana leaves, rather than corn husks. I will never forget those tamales. Mine had a big spine bone in it and I almost broke my tooth. If you are not expecting to find something hard in your food, you bite differently than you do if you expect bones, so I bit it pretty hard. Not only did I arrive achingly full, but I also was obligated to eat tamales with a bone surprise. I never ate tamales the same way again. It makes me full just to think of that night.

On New Year's Day Hector showed me four or five bullet shells that he found on my roof after the previous night's celebration. I didn't realize the part that bullets would play in my Acapulco experiences for some time, but they certainly did. At Rosy's house we heard a lot of gunfire, but it was difficult to distinguish from firecrackers. I still can't distinguish gunshots from firecrackers, it's not like on TV.

Stolen Passport

Rosy and I maintained contact and our friendship grew. One day she came to my apartment. She was dating a married guy who she was head-over-heels in love with, Diego. I was not very romantically interested in her, at the time I was very selective about the women I wanted to date, and she had Diego, so we were destined to be only friends, with one regrettable exception about five years later. We spent some time together talking at my apartment and then we got her a taxi and she went home.

I had a frantic, probably alcohol related, moment in which I thought my passport was gone, later that night. I looked and looked and looked for it. I could not find it for the life of me even though I had put it wherever it was. I finally got it into my head that she had grabbed it. What a moron, I so wish I had taken the whole situation slower. I called her and, in the most indirect way I could, accused her of taking it. She denied it and was understandably angry and upset. I continued to search for it and eventually found it between some disc golf discs in my closet. What an airhead. I was overcome with shame. I called her and she wouldn't take my call. I explained myself to her mom, but she couldn't get Rosy to answer. I was distressed.

I decided to take matters into my own hands and go to her house by myself. I had never gone there alone before. I got a bus that dropped me off in her neighborhood, under a bridge I recognized from the time I'd gone there before. I was nearby, but nearly clueless as to how to find her house. I was trying to use a pay phone to call her, but for some reason, wasn't getting it done. I was lost and a little stranded. It was dark and there were few streetlights.

Then, out of the shadows, a cop, sporting a heavy weapon, a rifle like most Mexican cops carry, starts talking to me. He remembers me from somewhere but I don't remember him. He reminded me where we had met and I recalled the occasion, my face recognition skills in Acapulco were always pretty bad. Somehow, between him, me, and the pay phone we got directions and I made it to the house. I trudged up the poorly paved, broken road that went about half way up, eventually turning into a dirt pathway.

I had taken a small banana bread my mom baked as a peace offering, I had brought it from Chicago shortly before that. The bread warmed Rosy's heart, my effort showed I was sincere, and my repentance soothed her mind and we remain friends to this day. One day in the not too distant future, I was to have one of my worst experiences in Acapulco with her.

Catfight

A few years later, Rosy and Diego married, however the zebra had not lost his stripes.

One fateful day Rosy called me up. She said she wanted me to accompany her to go and confront another cousin, who had been sleeping with Diego. I resisted, the idea didn't sound very wise to me. Rosy convinced me she only wanted to talk to the other girl so I drove out to pick her up over near the *Renacimiento* neighborhood, on the outskirts of town, where she was living. Helping her was a truly terrible decision, when you take an angry Acapulcan woman to confront her husband's lover, it's never a good thing. The bottom line is, I did it, and I paid for it for months and months to come.

The place where this girl lived was called *La Vacacional*, another one of those dangerous areas on the outskirts of Acapulco in the vicinity of *La Sabana* and *Renacimiento*. *La Vacacional* has one, and only one, main entrance and exit, which Rosy should have mentioned before we arrived for this encounter.

After stopping to call the girl to confirm that she was home, we drove to her house and knocked on her door. She came outside and they started talking, but this quickly devolved into arguing. To make the whole situation more absurd, Rosy was pregnant with Diego's child, not an ideal moment to go and fight with her husband's lover. Unsurprisingly, they each got aggressive and started fighting. I grabbed Rosy and blocked the other girl from hitting her. We all moved toward the car, avoiding blows as much as possible, and Rosy got in. I left the girl standing there screaming and we took off. Rosy later lauded the fact that I had saved her baby. I could have helped her even more by not taking her there in the first place. Rosy's daughter is sweet and adorable and physically fit, I'm glad to say.

In our haste to get away from the violent and angry cousin, and because the car was already facing that way, we drove away in the opposite direction from which we had entered. We traveled a few blocks and Rosy enlightened me to the fact that there is only one entrance and one exit to *La Vacacional*. We had to turn around and pass by the cousins' house again to get out. My Celica couldn't pass by that girl's house again without being seen. This was not a good situation. By chance, Rosy had more relatives who lived a few blocks down. We went to their house and a few of them agreed to escort us to the neighborhood exit in their car. It was a tense situation, I didn't want anyone to get hurt, and I was worried my car would get fucked up over this absurdity.

To reduce the possibility that the cousin would attack my car, and to throw her off Rosy's scent, Rosy got into the other car driven by her cousin. When we passed by, the girl was nowhere to be seen, it seemed the danger was over.

Then came the inevitable "but". We had half a mile to go before leaving the neighborhood. A few blocks down the road I stopped to let Rosy get back in the car with me. I pulled over to the side of the street and BAM. The right side of my car fell into a huge, gaping void. I could not go forward. I could not go backward. I was nowhere near the bottom, my wheel was not touching ground. Excavated for underground sewer work, there was a deep, large crater, unmarked in any way, along the curb of an otherwise well paved roadway.

It was like a bad movie. Someone is in a dangerous situation trying to escape a threat, they get away and then their escape is blocked. There were four of us trying to get the car out, a guy who rode with me and two others who had been in the car Rosy rode in. We had to try to lift the car out of the hole or push it enough so it got traction to get out of the hole. It was getting dark, the car could not be pulled out, and I was terrified of leaving my car in that neighborhood. Suddenly a guy arrived who proved to be my savior. He put some rocks under the wheel and they almost gave it traction as I tried driving the car out again. Then he gave the car an extra big shove and it came out of the hole. We were back on the road to safety.

I know I was very lucky the car wasn't damaged beyond drivability, as we drove away it seemed pretty normal. It wasn't. Part of the axle was broken. I don't remember specifics, why dwell on the awful. I know I took the car for repairs at least five times for the damage that occurred that day. It was hard to diagnose the problem, it seemed to just get worse and worse. I had to mail big auto parts from Chicago to Acapulco because none were available for my car there. I spent over $1200 on the repairs. It was an expensive experience. Rosy never even knew that the accident had caused me so much difficulty. It was an unforgettable, regrettable adventure.

Rosy and Hija

Tres Palos Lagoon

Another day Rosy invited me to go to a lagoon called Tres Palos where her uncle had a small house. I was always concerned about driving my car into areas where it was possible it would be damaged or stuck because of poor, or non-existent, roads. This day would be another test.

I drove to *La Sabana* and picked up Rosy. Then we went to a cousin's house, (she has a very large family), and picked up her sister and brother. Eventually we reached seven people in my car, more than ever before or since.

We drove a half hour to the rural area around the lagoon. The roads became dirt and were pocked, in some sections, with deep grooves, and holes, which had formed from rainfall and vehicle traffic. It was slow going. The car got heavily covered with fine dust. I have always had faith in my Celica and that day it proved its worth once again. Regardless of the heavy passenger load and the barely existent roads, we made it to our destination without incident. We had fun hanging out on the banks of the lagoon. One of Rosy's cousins scaled a coconut tree and got fresh coconuts for us. This time my day with Rosy was not to end in disaster.

The final time I saw Rosy was on Avenida Universidad , close to Tacos Chemis, Paco's old taco stand, and the Mega Commercial Mexicana supermarket. She was finishing her teaching degree and was on her way to the main union offices located near there. We talked about getting together, but never did.

Maru, Models, and the Super Bowl Pool

In February of 2004 I went to a Super Bowl party at Referee's, a sports bar I frequented at the time. It was convenient to walk to and they had cable that got Cubs games. There were enough TVs that it was usually possible to get them to tune in whatever game you wanted to watch. At the party everyone was picking numbers and putting money on a board, a betting pool. I picked one and paid 100 pesos. The first quarter was about to end and one of my numbers was "0", so there was a higher chance that it would win since one team had not yet scored. There was a minute and a half left, or so. Well, who won that pot? I did. I won 1,000 pesos. I was drinking, I was smoking, I hardly knew what the hell the pool was, I had just put my money down. So, the powers that be, the bar owner and his wife, Maru, decided I had placed my bet too late and they wouldn't give me my prize. That was the first contact I had with Maru. She was a very pretty woman, much younger than her husband. She owned a modeling agency. We crossed paths a number of times over the years, often with a questionable result for me.

A few months after that, I was with Felipe Rico and somehow we ended up at a party at Maru's on the roof of her hotel. That night Maru introduced me to a number of her models. We had a fine dinner on the terrace on top of the hotel, a block from the beach. It was an elegant setting, the area is expansive, with a small pool, an archway, and a stage area. I imagine some pretty famous people have been there over the years.

As the evening progressed, the moment arrived when these two very cute women and Maru wanted to go out. Since I had the best car in all of Acapulco, I was more than happy to take them all with me. It was the perfect combination. On the way these super sexy women were sitting up on the back seats of my car while we had the top down. I didn't get a good vibe from them, but it was a truly memorable moment, even if they were just there to mooch. After driving around for a while, they decided they wanted to go to Palladium, a popular nightclub on the "Escénica" road. I had never been there, I knew they charged about $30 cover and I rarely pay that much to get in to a place without a good band playing. I reluctantly acquiesced.

It turned out it cost $35 to get in and they wanted me to pay for two of them. I had enough for two, but that left one man out, the man being me. I felt foolish with these stunning women, and little cash, but I didn't want to pay over $100 to get into a club with three women I was feeling no connection to. Their idea was that I would pay for them, they would go in and, eventually, come out to get me once they found someone they knew who'd comp me in. Terrible idea. I threw down most of the cash I had on me so they could enter and left. My opinion of Maru dropped further.

The last time I saw her was in mid-2010 in front of the Universidad Americana where I had worked, a half block from her hotel. She wanted my number to try to hook me up with someone, I told her I had no phone.

Maru and Me

Sexy Chicas on Celica's Backseat

Return to the Scene of the Crime

Monday, March 28th, 2011

After my abrupt departure in January, I still had to get all my worldly possessions out of Acapulco. I was quite reluctant to go back there after the life-threatening phone call, but I had my car, my albums, my furniture, my clothes, much of my stereo equipment, and many more things that I wasn't about to abandon there until I eventually made it back.

I arranged to have a moving company meet me there a day after I arrived. They would take two days to pack up and leave with all my stuff. They guaranteed me very little about how long it would take, passing one's worldly possessions through Mexican and U.S. Customs is expensive, slow, and especially difficult, if the owner is not with them. This move cost well over twice as much as it had cost me to move down there. Part of the reason was my car. I refused to drive the highways of Mexico again, and shipping my car would cost about $6,000, more than it was technically even worth. All told, this move cost over $12,000. People told me I could just buy new stuff for the same amount of money. It would have been impossible to replace my things. Moreover, I did not want to be responsible for the consumption of so much stuff when I already had the things I had.

The day I was flying back I went to lunch with Joe at Pita Inn. After eating I went to Lou Malnati's to get frozen pizzas to take with me. I bought a plain cheese for the first time ever, which saved my ass in Mexico City when they searched my luggage. The rules had recently changed, passengers went through customs in Mexico City, rather than Acapulco, and things were a little more strict. Travelers were not allowed to enter the country with meat. The agents saw the pizzas, but the one they asked about contained no meat, so I told the truth when I said it did not. I didn't mention that the other one was pepperoni.

While driving to the airport, I missed my turn off of Interstate 294 and had to drive eight extra miles, 20+ minutes, in order to leave the expressway and head back to where I was going to park. GPS saved my ass, (after fucking me up in the first place). I arrived at Pride Parking, dropped off my car, climbed aboard the shuttle, and got to O'Hare at 2:05, for my flight at 3:55.

The line moved more smoothly than any I had experienced in a long time, kudos, Aeromexico staff. I bought an upgrade because it was a pretty good deal, and business class is always nice.

Part of my luggage was one of my custom-made wooden boxes, crafted by Plutarco, my Acapulcan carpenter. After checking in I took it over to the men who would pass it through the baggage x-ray machine. The middle-aged white guy at security was kind of freaked out, but he managed to open it, found it half empty, and sealed it again with his own screwdriver, I had brought one just in case.

I went to one VIP lounge, only to find that it was no longer for use by Aeromexico customers. The woman there directed me to the correct one at the other end of the terminal. It was the Air France Lounge, shared by Aeromexico. Arriving to the greeting, "bon jour", I went in and had a Jack Daniels and Diet Pepsi, and some cheese and crackers. After another Jack and diet, I made my way back to the gate as general boarding was beginning.

Service onboard was mediocre, at best, but the flight went fine.

Arriving in Acapulco at just after 10 p.m., I was picked up by an acquaintance who drives a taxi, he was driving his own car because of rules at the airport about who can legally, officially, pick up fares and who can't. If he had been driving a taxi he would not have been allowed to pick me up.

As we drove down the road about a half mile from the airport we got to a spot where the police were doing an *operativo*, a revision of random cars. There were at least ten police vehicles, cruisers, pick up trucks, and more. In and around them there were at least 60 police officers. I was dreading getting stopped and having them see the custom-made wooden box, it was completely innocuous, but its singularity would certainly have attracted attention. This was a truly frightening moment. Sometimes luck is on your side and it was on ours that night, they let us pass without stopping.

I was paranoid that during my brief five-day stay there'd be a big earthquake and I'd be stuck there. My cats were in my small hotel room at the Comfort Inn in Skokie, alone. On the morning after I arrived one of the longest temblors I ever experienced occurred. It was not too strong, but it seemed to go on forever. One geological movement often follows another so this did not bode well.

In January, the day after I got the threatening phone call, I went to the Telmex office to tell them about the call. While there, I made a boneheaded decision and only changed my phone number rather than suspending the line, too. I had a hefty $250.00 phone bill waiting for me when I went back in March. This meant I had no Internet or phone at home. I wasn't about to pay so much money to have my phone connected for a few days while I was there. My neighbor, Dolores, gave me access to her network, but my iPad couldn't connect due to the distance between apartments. I was left without even basic connectivity in my secluded abode.

As soon as I got there I started packing. The movers were going to pack the big stuff, but I had to do some of it and I had to gather the things I wanted to take back myself. I was planning to take all my albums with me in the boxes Plutarco made for me, but I ended up shipping them with the movers for many reasons, including the fact that they weighed a ton. If I had had to take them myself, they would've been a challenge to get to the airport and, during travel, would've been subject to the treatment of the baggage handlers.

While making the final arrangements for the move, I opened my big mouth and told my contact at the moving company that my street was pretty narrow. Because the truck they were sending was 20 meters long and my street is impossible to enter with a vehicle of that size, they jacked up the price by

$1500.00 MXN ($150.00 USD). I got the feeling that they wouldn't have charged me for that if I hadn't told them ahead of time, I'll never know.

The first day, movers arrived at 7:30 a.m. to measure the amount, and size, of the things I was sending so they could bring the necessary packing materials. Thank goodness I had Dolores send a *croquis*, (sketch), of the area, she had made an exceptional one previously, it always worked. It would've been very hard to communicate with the movers to navigate them in, having no phone or Internet. My street is nearly impossible to locate if you don't know where you're going.

I spent the whole day packing. I had plans with Miguel and Miguel and had to leave to pick up Miguel, "El Tocayo", before the movers were ready to leave, so I asked them to wrap it up and finish the next day. They wouldn't have finished that day anyway. One guy took at least an hour to wrap my 20 year old exercise bike that is worth $50.00, at best. They disassembled tables and chairs that could have shipped whole. Clearly they were being paid by the hour.

That night we ended up at El Morro, Neftalí's family's restaurant. We polished off a 1.75L bottle of Bacardi Blanco, sharing it with quite a few people we knew, I saw ten people I know, if not more. Acapulco is like a small town inside a big city. There was a great salsa band playing, some of whom were Cubans. Live salsa, great food, and friends on the beach in Acapulco can't be beat.

Journal Notes: Packing

Here I am in Acapulco drinking rum, (first with Diet Coke now with purple Gatorade). I set my iPod to play all songs starting from the letter "A", (I reached 10,198 songs today, first time ever over 10,000, so the odds of playing a specific song are slim), and what song comes on but this one, "Ain't this the Life", Oingo Boingo, from 1979. Tonight I saw one of the best fireworks shows I recall, directly in front of my apartment, (usually they're off to the left), while overseeing the move of my belongings.

"Holiday in Spain" by Counting Crows always reminds me of a time shortly after I moved to Acapulco. I was living on Calle Fiji at the top of Calle Bora Bora. I was lying on my balcony and I had no food in the house except some bananas. I had exactly one bottle of tequila. All of a sudden my computer, (iPods were not on my radar in '03), plays "Holiday in Spain" and I hear Adam Duritz say "got a couple of bananas and a bottle of booze". Amusing coincidence. Sometimes my iPod is prophetic.

I just got home from my favorite hangout, Zydeco. Three months and 10 days ago my buddy Fernando was gunned down 50 yards from where we were drinking and partying and eating Lou Malnati's Pizza an hour ago. Pretty bizarre. Here's what happened that day.

Afternoon Assassination

I met Fernando Galeana on December 18, 2009 at Monasterio, a bar near the *Condesa* area in Acapulco. His girlfriend Jahzeel, my date Johana's sister, worked there. We drank and talked and got to know each other a bit. I liked him immediately. He impressed me as a very friendly, intelligent person. He was a lawyer.

The next time I saw him was also at Monasterio, I went there with Johana, who was my girlfriend by then. We all caroused for a while and had a good time together. That night I met his associate, Elias, as well as some other folks. One of the guys was flirting a lot with Johana, as were some women who were there, too, but Fernando was respectful.

A month later I saw him at Johana's' daughter's birthday party, which we celebrated at Johana's brother's house. Fernando got there very late, he was always working. Once again, hanging with him, the night was fun and the conversation stimulating.

A number of weeks later, I was at a bar called Yardas. I went there to see a band that I had seen, met, and partied with nearby, at La Crissis, a few weeks earlier. Fernando was sitting a few tables down from me and invited me to join his group. He was with Johana's nutty sister and another couple. When the other couple left, the three of us went to La Crissis together to see more live music. Eventually Jahzeel left and Fernando and I got to talk man to man, *concuño* to *concuño*, (we were dating sisters, a *concuño* is a man who is married to your wife's sister, but the term is used in reference to less formal relationships, too). When the talk turned to drugs I told him I was looking for some pot. He knew a one-stop-shop, so to speak, a two-minute drive away, and took me to buy some bud while he scored some coke for himself. I was quite familiar with the street we went to, but not aware that drugs were sold there at night. One of my favorite taco carts set up there in the daytime.

During my stay in Acapulco I never had a good connection for pot, so when he offered to take me to get some I jumped at the chance. Although it was a little tense, and the sellers didn't recognize him at first because he was driving a different car than usual, in short order we took care of business and were on our way.

While we were at La Crissis we had a very frank talk about him, his girlfriend, and her daughter. Jahzeel is the most un-attentive mother I've ever met. She is very irresponsible and lazy, and Fernando and I were both disturbed by this. We agreed that it seemed we both cared more about her daughter than she did. It was disheartening, and frustrating, for each of us to see things that way.

Fernando was the most educated and intelligent person I ever met in Acapulco. It was evident in every conversation we had. He told me about how he had taken the equivalent of the Bar Exam in Mexico City. The other people waiting there to take it were giving him a hard time for being from Acapulco where education is generally poor. Acapulcans are frowned upon by some other

Mexicans. When results were distributed, it turned out that he had earned the highest score of all examinees, which put his critics in their place.

Over the course of our conversation I told him about my passion for disc golf and that my wish was to play on the area around the Acapulco Convention Center which was ideal for the game. He was up for giving it a try, but because the grounds were closed, and fenced off, doing so would have been a little tricky. In the end we never got the chance to play.

On April 15th I got a phone call from Johana. We had spoken the day before, shortly after a prolonged, and disturbing, shooting occurred on the main strip, in the middle of the afternoon, about a half a mile from my apartment. As the events unfolded all the people around my building, including me, looked down toward the apparent source of the confrontation. The guys who were working on the roof next to my apartment all ducked down or got on their knees while the shooting occurred. I wasn't sure if it was firecrackers or gunshots, but I found out pretty soon that it was the latter.

This was the most public, horrific, and alarming shooting to date in Acapulco. It happened at 3:30 in the afternoon in front of the new shopping mall, Galerías, in the middle of the main tourist zone, almost directly in front of my hangout, Zydeco.

When Johana called me the next day the first thing she said was, "It was Fer". I didn't hear her well. She repeated it and I went cold. I couldn't believe it. I didn't think he was involved in selling drugs, and I still don't. Jahzeel told us that he was working on a real estate deal that involved one of the notorious drug lords. No one knows what he did, or what they thought he did, but he was chased down the Costera and gunned down. 40 rounds were found in his body when the autopsy was performed.

Fernando and Me

Chase

These events are recreated through firsthand knowledge of details surrounding them, combined with speculation about what must have taken place.

It is about 2:00 p.m. on Wednesday, April 14, 2010, coincidentally, the 145th anniversary of the day that Abraham Lincoln was shot. My friend Fernando is expected back at his apartment, (hardly more than a room), by Jahzeel, his girlfriend. He calls her to say that he's been delayed, he is going to help an associate with a business matter that should be brief. This associate is known to Jahzeel, she has told Fernando that she is uncomfortable with the man and that she doesn't want him to interact with him. For reasons unknown, financial?, generosity?, willingness to help a friend?, Fernando does not heed her request. Instead of going home to his woman, he agrees to accompany this man, or men, on an errand that was not to require too much of his time this afternoon. They pick him up and head west, toward El Zocalo, rather than east, toward his room.

After completing the errand somewhere near El Zocalo, they begin to drive back west toward Fernando's apartment, presumably so they can drop him off at home.

At an indeterminate point in time, and space, possibly near the *asta bandera*, (the 50 foot high flag pole with a gigantic Mexican flag flying at Papagayo Beach), the two men in the car become aware that their lives are in danger. They are being followed. Their pursuers are extremely violent and dangerous men. Did something happen at the meeting that incited anger and violent rage? Did they know the people who were following them? Were shots fired en route to the scene of the crime? We may never know.

Traffic is heavy, eluding attackers would take extraordinary luck and maneuvering. The chase doesn't traverse more than a half mile of the Costera. It ends on the corner in front of the Hacienda Maria Eugenia hotel, just before the Galerías shopping mall, at a traffic light.

In Acapulco the Costera Miguel Alemán runs the entire length of the bay, about three miles. For the majority of the distance there is a median that divides the two directions of travel. In Spanish it is called a *camellón*, which translates to "traffic island", coincidentally their shape is reminiscent of a camel. Topographically these islands are very similar to actual islands. At intersections they tend to be flat and paved, but mid-street, they are lined with palm trees and bushes and are covered with grass. They are also quite steep, forming an elongated hump, peaking at two feet of height, or more. If the grass is wet, the slippery slope can be a struggle. It's not uncommon to see dirt troughs dug out at points along the way where foot traffic has worn the hill down to allow easier passage across.

Most traffic lights along the strip have left turn arrows, and a short stretch of roadway, where those making a left turn can move out of the main traffic lane, narrowing or eliminating the *camellón* at that point. Traffic lights in Acapulco may last longer than two full minutes, so when you are stopped, you are *very* stopped. It is not uncommon to find a variety of salespeople trolling the lines of cars selling their wares, others may blow flames from their mouth or lay a bed of glass shards on the ground and lie down on it, all in hopes of collecting a few pesos. Most common are the window washers who are notorious for making your window dirtier than it was when you stopped at the light. They walk along, spraying windshields before less observant drivers can waive them off, then proceed to clean off the glass. The water they use has little soap and often leaves dirty streaks.

Two pick-up trucks chase Fernando's car from behind, the men inside race for their lives. When they get close to the Emporio Hotel, police SUVs come from the opposite direction. Hundreds of rounds of gunfire are exchanged as the police realize what is going down and fire upon the vehicles pursuing Fernando. In an urgent attempt to flee the assault, the driver of Fernando's vehicle jams the accelerator, turns the steering wheel and tries desperately to cross the precipitous median, only to be detained by the barrage of bullets ripping through the car. The police who arrive from the opposite direction engage in an extensive gun battle with Fernando's pursuers. Six people die and at least five others are injured.

Traffic stops for over an hour and bullet riddled cars are abandoned at the scene. This area that I had traversed dozens of times became an impromptu war zone.

Aftermath of the Shootout

Thor's Murder

Another tragedy occurred precisely 13 weeks after Fernando was killed. It was Wednesday, July 7, 2010 at about 3:45 p.m. and my friend Fred's brother Thor was just getting off work. He was a Chicago police officer who was highly respected and beloved by his fellow officers. He was teaching an advanced training class in a dangerous neighborhood on the south side. As he left the station he was confronted by a crazy man in the parking lot. Somehow in the struggle the guy managed to wrestle Thor's gun from him. He shot Thor dead right there. I learned about this the next day as I watched the WGN News at noon in my apartment in Acapulco. The irony was not lost on me of the fact that these two men, friends of mine to varying degrees, had been murdered at virtually the same time, on the same day of the week, with just over three months transpiring between events. They were both good people, taken from us with the ultimate equalizer, guns. Thor was 43 years old.

In September of 2015 Thor's killer was sentenced to life in prison plus 115 years.

Chicago Police Officer Thor Soderberg, Star #14767, was murdered while returning to his vehicle at the end of his tour of duty. The vehicle was located in the parking lot of the police facility at 61st Street and Racine Avenue. While in that parking lot, the uniformed officer became involved in a struggle with a 24-year old male individual. During the struggle, the offender fatally shot him.

Officer Soderberg joined the Chicago Police Department in August 1999 and was most recently assigned to the Education and Training Division. He is survived by his wife.

Thor

Chivo Returns

Cats have been a big part of my life since December of 1996 when my ex-wife Angélica and I adopted Hamlet. We found him at the Anti-Cruelty Society in downtown Chicago. A friend of Angélica's had asked us to cat-sit for her but her trip was canceled so we didn't. We had become excited about the idea of having a cat, so we adopted Hamlet, (no Shakespearean reference). He was about three months old. It seemed he picked me, he clung to me pretty quickly and it was love at first sight. He and I have been through a hell of a lot, two broken legs, one deep, forceful bite on my wrist, and 3.5 trips roundtrips by car to Mexico, he's a good sport. Probably one of the world's most traveled cats.

The next cats I got I found in Zihuatanejo in January of 2003, within weeks of moving to Acapulco; Chivo, Zihua and Kitty. Classes did not begin at the university until the 20th of the month, so I had time to travel a bit before beginning the semester. I was staying at the Hotel Zihua. There were four kittens living by the flower box outside the hotel lobby door. They were mere days old and, as kittens tend to be, adorable.

The hotel staff chased them off to the other side of the street, next to a fence and vacant lot. Three of them wouldn't stay away, they went back to hide behind the flower box and I saw them again. I had already spoken to my landlords and they said I could have a cat, so taking one back to Acapulco with me was not a problem. I couldn't decide which one I wanted and it broke my heart to leave them there, so I took all three. The cheapest, most accessible carrier option was a box that was intended for *gallos de pelea*, (fighting roosters). Everyone who saw me with the box thought I was carrying roosters. Whatever the case, they all fit well in the box, they were tiny. The fourth one wouldn't let me near him, so he stayed there. Kitty died when they were neutering him, at five months of age. Zihua and I parted ways after a few years and Chivo is still with me now.

In August 2005 I was moving back to Chicago and didn't want to travel with four cats. Three is hard enough. So I had to get rid of either Zihua, Chivo or Lucky. Lucky was still quite young and we got along well, I hadn't had her for long. Until the very last moment, I wasn't sure which cat I would give away, Zihua or Chivo. I must have had a much better relationship with Zihua than I did later on, because she reached a point where she barely let me touch her. Chivo used to climb up the slatted windows in my apartment and climb out through open slats high up the wall, he was not very affectionate.

Carlos Varela had a neighbor, Arturo, who wanted a cat, so I gave him Chivo. They say let your love go and it will return, and Chivo came back to me. I hate to imagine what he lived through during the two days he was gone, I think he spent it in his carrier. When Arturo brought him back, he was filthy. He has had a terror of carrying cases since then, but he's an amazingly sweet kitty and lives up to his name by being a consummate bug, lizard, and bird eater. He is a hunter and has killed more than his share of *cuijas*, (small lizards), cockroaches, other bugs, and a couple of birds. He loved going outside in Acapulco when I would let him. He would come back with pupils dilated and a weird kind of energy, but the day came when I worried too much about his safety and possible contact with illness so I stopped letting him go outside.

Why did Chivo get returned? Let me preface it by saying, he was neutered at about three or four months of age. He was returned because Arturo's mother said he was pregnant. He still hasn't given birth, but his midsection does look like a barrel, and his stomach bulges out at the base of his ribs. I am eternally grateful he came back, he is a very special cat.

My fourth Mexican kitty was Lucky, who I had for a few years. She climbed up into my car one morning at about 5:00 a.m. when I was dropping Carlos off in his parking lot. I thought she was lucky and, frankly, she was very lucky. She now lives in Wilmette, Illinois with a nice woman named Heather. Lucky would almost certainly have died years ago if she had remained on the streets of Acapulco. We didn't get along too well when she matured, I have no idea why. I gave her to Heather, who worked at my bank. She is the only cat in Heather's house. I think that was critical to her happiness, so it was the best outcome possible that she ended up with her. I ran into Heather one night in 2011, Lucky is still with her and doing well.

I left Zihua with Carlos Varela. He let her out and she stopped coming home. I'm sorry Zi! In the end she didn't like for me to touch her, not a pleasant relationship to have with your pet. She and Carlos got along much better than she and I.

I found Squeaky at the mouth of my street, in a flower box. The box was more than a foot off the ground and he was no more than five inches long. He could barely walk and his eyes were barely open. It was obvious that someone intentionally put him up in that box, it was physically impossible for him to get up there on his own. He was making a sound that I thought was a small bird, I walked right by without paying much attention. Upon my return, I heard the same chirping sound. I stopped and looked and there was a teeny tiny Squeaky. I took him home and investigated what to feed him, I knew cats are not supposed to drink cow milk, so I didn't want to give him that. I gave him minuscule chunks of raw chicken. He didn't grow very fast. For months after I found him I was sure he'd be the smallest cat on Earth.

He was about the size of a medium-sized rat. He fit in the palm of my hand. I kept him under a lamp to try to keep him warm, the air was about 85 degrees during the day, but the wind kept it cooler. I wanted him to be warm, he had very little skin and fur on his bones. At night the temperatures were lower so it was especially important I keep heat on him then.

When he was four or five months old he was still tiny. I thought he was eating well, I was giving him as much food as he seemed to want. When he finally began to eat cat food, he grew and grew and grew. Looking at him today it would be impossible to guess that he was so small for so long. He's an above average sized cat. During the first months of his life, I was constantly on the lookout for anyone's feet to get too close to him. He would not have survived being stepped on.

When he was no more than two weeks old, a scorpion, the only one I ever saw inside my apartment, (as opposed to the others I had seen on the outside stairway or on my terrace), came into my kitchen and went under my stove. I was freaked out. I couldn't have that thing walking around my apartment. I saw him go under my stove so I summoned my courage, moved the stove, took a fly swatter and smacked the hell out of him as soon as I saw the whites of his eyes.

At that time, in 2006, I was living in Chicago, and was only in Acapulco on vacation. I had never taken any cat on an airplane before. I was certain I needed some documents to make everything legal. Having him vaccinated was not an option, he weighed less than one pound. I took him to my veterinarian who gave me a piece of paper indicating he was in good health. Documents are king in Mexico and this was my only hope for making his health status official for international travel. I expected customs in Chicago to want to see proof he was healthy, also.

In 2006 the quantity of flights between Chicago and Acapulco was diminished from the previous years. There were either two or three a week. If I missed my scheduled flight it would mean I'd have to wait two or three days until the next direct flight out of Acapulco. I did not want to travel with a connecting flight, nor did I want to go back to my condo and wait two days for the next flight.

I assumed it would not be necessary to get a real pet carrier because Squeaky was so small he could easily climb out of the hole meant for the cat or dog's head. I rigged a cloth bag with Velcro to keep it partially closed while allowing plenty of air to enter. If he had been in a small cage he would've been rolling around it because he was still unstable on his feet. I arrived at the airport very early, thank goodness. My friend Cesar worked for Mexicana Airlines and I thought that if he were the one who checked me in it might mean some rules could be bent. Unfortunately, the airline required me to use a regulation pet carrier. I had to leave Squeaky with them to go buy one as quickly as possible. The airport in Acapulco is not very close to any major shopping area where there would be a pet store.

According to the airline staff, the nearest place where there was a possibility of getting one was at a housing complex called El Colosio, roughly two miles from the airport. I had very little cash, so I decided to take a bus, I could be back in less than an hour if things went right. It was about 90 degrees and quite humid out. The bus was supposed to take me to the entrance of the neighborhood and drop me off, from there I would walk a block or two to the pet store. I asked the driver to let me know when we got there. After riding for what seemed too long, I asked the driver where I should get off, again. We were already a quarter mile past it. Now I had to backtrack three or four blocks, then go a few blocks into the neighborhood complex. I eventually found the pet store. It was over half a mile from where I got off the bus.

They had a very small selection of pet carriers. The one I ended up buying appeared slightly used, it was unwrapped, but it was the only one they had that was anything close to what I needed. It had flowers on it and it was bright pink.

Squeaky could easily climb right out of it, the openings were for a normal sized pet. I grabbed the first cab I saw and made it back to the airport in time for my flight. The new bag worked, I got on, I made it to Chicago with him on what was one of no more than a half dozen non-stop flights I ever took between Acapulco and Chicago. Now non-stops don't even exist.

While carrying Squeaky in that bag, I had no guarantee that he would not climb out of it at any time, I didn't keep him in it much of the time for exactly that reason, so I could not sleep or rest with him under my watch. But, I was fortunate to have a young girl next to me on the flight who held him and played with him for a good portion of the time. He was happy, she was happy, and I was happy.

Miraculously they let Squeaky pass with no documents. He continues to be a miracle to this day and weighs 15 times what he weighed when I found him.

Raining Cats

One night in 2004 something awful happened to Hamlet. Inés and I had gone downstairs after spending the evening on my terrace, he remained up there by himself. I had no reason to think he would be at risk of falling, there is a two foot high wall bordering the entire area and I had never seen him even try to get up onto it, let alone jump from there. I imagine he saw a bird, or a bat, and leaped to try to catch it. He fell 35-40 feet to my neighbor's roof.

After a while I noticed that he was missing. Some scary moments passed when I had no idea where he was until I realized he had landed on my neighbor's roof. Their house is built on uneven ground so getting onto the top of it is fairly easy in certain areas, I could climb up to where he was to get him down. His chin was bloodied and his leg was broken. At eight years of age he was more susceptible to injury. Generally he was in good health, until then his worst moment had been when he broke a leg after getting startled and slamming his leg on a table, immediately jumping onto it, on the floor. He recovered from that incident with not so much as a limp.

Hamlet's travels back and forth between Chicago and Acapulco by car totaled more than 11,000 miles, (17,700 km). He is as active as one might expect now that he is 17 years and, other than a limp from his second broken leg, has no permanent injuries from the fall.

Wrist Chomp

One day, when I was living with Humberto and Señora Silvia, their cat was outside my apartment, visible through the full length kitchen window. My apartment comprised the top floor of the building. In the kitchen there were some vertical blinds, held together by a thin, beaded, metal chain at the bottom. Hammy was observing, and possibly interacting with, the cat through the glass, they were eyeing each other for a few minutes and then he got excited and became entangled in the chain. When I saw his predicament I tried to free him. He may have been sexually aroused, and in the heat of the moment, bit me with the full force of his jaws.

I don't remember any pain, but I was bleeding everywhere. I guess the shock of the whole situation kind of numbed me. I didn't know what to do. My wrist swelled up to more than double its normal size, it was huge. I was scared shitless. I finally got in my car, after walking through my landlord's living room to get to the street, and drove down the mountain to where Paco's taco stand was. Paco and I decided the best way to deal with the problem was to go to the fire station a few blocks away. We drove over and the paramedics looked me over. They took me into an emergency vehicle, combination ambulance and fire truck, where they had access to their supplies. They gave me a tetanus shot and bandaged my arm. I was fortunate to have a friend to help me through that, it's one of very few times I've been suddenly injured to that degree.

A few months later I got dengue fever. Dengue is pretty similar to flu, although there are cases that are more severe than others. It gives you body aches and chills and nausea, kind of saps all your energy. Up north where I grew up, dengue is not often an issue. My dengue was not so severe, I was slowly recovering after spending a few days at home alone, suffering through it. The second or third day I had to go to the vet to buy cat food. When I mentioned my illness, she told me how to deal with it, so a fireman cured my cat bite and a vet cured my dengue.

Chivo, Hamlet, Zihua and Señora Silvia's Cat

Chivo, Hamlet, Lucky, and Tiny Squeaky

Lucky's Plunge

Not long after I found her, Lucky fell from my terrace to the side opposite from where Hamlet fell, the east side. There is no house there, only a back patio. It is at least 60 feet down. I didn't hear her meowing. I had no idea exactly where she had gone.

Two days later my neighbors rang my bell and asked me if I had lost a cat. She was hiding on their patio. I happily retrieved her. She was completely unharmed, albeit very hungry.

Chivo Can't Be Contained

My Tiny Black Angel, Squeaky

Squeaky, King Sized

Down the Coast

In August of 2002, after having been in Acapulco for vacation twice that month, I returned to Chicago to begin the new school year, with my brand new Masters Degree in Bilingual/Bicultural Education. I was returning to Jordan Elementary School where I had been hired in January to take over a split bilingual class of 6th, 7th, and 8th graders.

I was soon informed that my class was to be mainstreamed into regular English classes. It may have been the fact that I was earning over $50,000, or because there weren't many students in my group that year, or both, whatever the reason, my classroom teacher position was being eliminated. I was given a new role as a "push-in/pull-out" teacher. I was expected to enter some classes and assist bilingual students in the classroom while another teacher taught the class. In other cases I would pull students out for personal tutoring to assist them with their general education, non-bilingual classes. Almost immediately, politics and bureaucracy reared their ugly heads again and this position was eliminated also.

At that point in time I had five years' experience in the classroom, my Masters Degree, and other teaching certificates. Some teachers in the same school were not certified with permanent certificates, and others had far less teaching experience than me. Since I had resigned, involuntarily, to do student teaching the previous year, I suddenly had zero seniority. I was out the door. It seemed to me that destiny was pushing me to fulfill my dream and move to Mexico.

I may have had a premonition about moving to Acapulco when I was there in August. I certainly had the desire to move there since a time long before my position was eliminated, but half the places I visit I want to move to, so this was far from unique.

When I was in Acapulco in August, I had done my best to make myself look employable with the casual summer wear I had packed. I then walked into the Universidad Americana de Acapulco and asked for a job. I was staying at a hotel that was about a block away and every time I walked past the university I tripped on the broken sidewalk in front of the campus. Eventually I managed to notice whose sidewalk was tripping me up all the time.

The university was beautifully designed. Its buildings were a reddish clay color especially chosen by the founders. The cobblestone path leading up to the principal structure was flanked by two decorative pools about 30 feet long by 15 feet wide. The main classroom area was built of stone and there was a 20 foot, pyramid-like, tapering, white granite stairway leading up to the central section of campus.

I got cleared by security and went in to speak to one of the rectors. He sent me to the Center for Foreign Language Studies at the rear of the campus. There I spoke to the department head and she told me that they would hire me if I moved to Acapulco. It was a very casual arrangement, but it was agreed that I would work there if I decided to reside in Mexico.

Trial Move

In September of 2002 I found myself without my major source of income and, after years of contemplating how nice it would be to live in a warm, sunny place, I finally decided to do it. I would leave the comfort of the place where I had lived my whole life, leave my condo, with a $1200 monthly mortgage, and an assessment of close to $300 a month, and go down to Mexico. I was teaching ESL at Truman College at the time. My students were intrigued, and sorry, that I was moving to Mexico. Many of them were Mexican immigrants, certainly they saw some irony in my moving south while they had all moved north.

Before I left I had to have a going away party. It was the last party I ever had that my parents attended. I was proud, to share my mom's baked goods with my friends, she was a phenomenal baker and her treats were always a big hit at every party I held. For this shindig I had her prepare cookies, cinnamon rolls, and other delicious desserts. Some ex-classmates from Northeastern came, as well as a lot of Truman students, University of Chicago mentors I had worked with, and other friends.

My plan was to stay in Mexico for six months to see how things went and decide whether I liked it enough to make the move permanent. It was imperative that I accumulate at least $50,000.00 worth of purchase points on my credit card before I left. I needed them to be able to buy my six-month ticket to Acapulco. The airlines did not offer a ticket with that length of stay, so purchasing the ticket normally, a full coach fare, would have been very, very expensive. For some reason, the credit card ticket had different rules.

In September, three months before I planned to depart, I was at about $48,000, lacking $2,000 to reach my goal. Then I had a brainstorm. I realized that I could buy gift cards from the major, local grocery stores and sell them to friends and family to reach the threshold. Their money would be tied up briefly until they, inevitably, shopped at one of the stores. I had no reason, or ability, to spend the amount of money needed to reach the minimum point level before I wanted to leave. Most people were very accommodating. At the party my friends took a bunch of gift cards off my hands.

My parents were diametrically opposed to my move from day one, so they made excuses for not buying more than a few cards from me. This was just the beginning of their unhappy attitude about the whole thing. Fortunately, I did reach the point level and got my ticket.

During the trial move I left my car in my garage in Evanston. I put most of my belongings in my second bedroom and rented my apartment to an ex-student of mine from Truman College. I charged her far less than what my apartment was worth and left my cat Hamlet in her care as part of the agreement. I had no place to stay while I looked for housing, so taking him on the plane with me and looking for lodging in a foreign country seemed like too much of a risk. When I returned in June, after the trial move, Hamlet looked obese, however the arrangement worked and Maria took good care of my condo and my cat.

In the months before I moved, I was remodeling my kitchen and bathroom, the building I lived in was close to 100 years old and an update was long overdue. One day they were ripping up the bathroom walls and about to put in new ones. I had to close Hamlet in a bedroom when I was at work, but could not locate him in any of his usual hiding spots. After minutes of desperation, I discovered him between the ripped out wall and the bathtub. If I hadn't found him, they could have sealed him up in there and he may never have been found. It was a real challenge to find him and we were both very lucky I got him out before the work was done. Ironically, it turned out that I only lived in the condo a few months after the remodel was finished.

In the weeks and months prior to my *viaje* I became aware of how many Acapulcan friends I had in Chicago. I have been a client at Frontera Grill here since they opened in 1987, so I knew some of their staff fairly well. Before I was to begin my adventure, I spoke to Fernando, a bartender there, who was from Acapulco. By chance his sister, Luz Maria, was going to be visiting Chicago just before my departure and was actually booked on the same flight as I was on her return. In 2002 there were four or five non-stop flights to Acapulco from Chicago per week. Nowadays there are none. Fernando's sister ended up facilitating the discovery of my first apartment and, later, the condominium I bought. She provided exactly the help I needed.

Luz Maria and I went to the airport together, sat side-by-side on the flight, and went looking for an apartment for me to rent once we arrived. We saw three places, two of which were almost as expensive to rent as an apartment in Chicago. I liked the last one which rented for $250 a month. It was built on top of the Maldonado family's house, accessible via an outside staircase to the rooftop. It was small, but had a nice view of the bay, and was in a neighborhood called *Magallanes*, (Magellan in English). All the streets there are named after islands around Fiji. Bora Bora was the main artery. I loved the name scheme, which I find interesting since Acapulco is hot like the South Pacific. My landlords owned a well located convenience store on a main street about a mile down the mountain near the Diana la Cazadora statue, (Diana the Hunter, a popular Acapulcan symbol). I lived in a total of three apartments in Acapulco and was never far from that area.

In late December 2002, just after moving in, I took a bus to Mexico City to spend Christmas with Karla and Hector, a married couple who I met through my ex-wife in Evanston, Illinois, in 1988. They were my best friends in Mexico for a long time. I had a close relationship with Karla, we liked the same music and got along well, but there always seemed to be an undertone of more than friendship between us. My feelings for Karla were entirely platonic. If I had wanted to get involved with her she would've been up for it, but I never wanted to and don't regret not having taken it to another level. Hector is my friend too, so I had even more reason for not having sex with her.

A few years later things got weird and I had to end contact with them. Karla was confiding things in me that I felt wrong about, (her infidelity and subsequent pregnancy by her lover), but couldn't tell to Hector because she told them to me in confidence. It was an uncomfortable, disturbing, situation.

Erick, Karla, and Hector

A Career in Teaching

I became an elementary school teacher in Chicago in 1996 after my sister-in-law told me Chicago Public Schools, (CPS), needed bilingual people with college degrees. I had been looking for a job and was pretty confident in my Spanish. Angélica and I had been together for more than seven years, so I had her as a live-in tutor, and I had worked for Iberia Airlines of Spain for five years, previously, so my Spanish was progressing well.

After navigating the bureaucratic juggernaut of CPS, and passing a difficult Spanish proficiency test, I was given a Transitional Bilingual Certificate which would allow me to teach Kindergarten through Eighth Grade for eight years. Two years later I decided to get a permanent certificate because I enjoyed teaching so much, I didn't want to give it up after my temporary certificate expired. I enrolled in a Masters program at Northeastern University, (NEIU), in Chicago. I studied hard for three years and earned certificates as a bilingual teacher, as well as an elementary level teacher. Simultaneously, I was taking some computer classes and Spanish classes so when I finished I jumped a lane to a masters +15 hours teaching level. Everything was fine. Or was it?

In order to complete the program I was required to resign from my teaching position, the one I had had for five full school years, to do my student teaching. Throughout the program my cadre of classmates and I were told by NEIU that the administration was working with the State of Illinois to get special status so teachers with significant classroom experience would be exempt from the student teaching requirement. Whether that was b.s. or just didn't go through I'll never know, but we were not exempted.

NEIU told me they would allow me to do my student teaching in my classroom if my principal would agree. The previous year I had switched from teaching fourth grade to teaching computer classes, 40 computer classes a week to grades one through eight. I was also in charge of maintenance of all the school's computers and peripherals. This encompassed the computer lab, all the computers in the main and annex buildings, plus five mobile classrooms. Enrollment was about 1,500 students at the time.

When the university realized that I was a computer teacher, they told me that this would not be acceptable for my student teaching. This was very upsetting news. Not only was I being required to work for a semester for free, but I would have to relinquish my computer lab, a position I enjoyed very much.

It was finally agreed that I could do my student teaching at the annex school, two blocks away, in a second grade classroom. This made maintaining the computers and fulfilling my student teaching responsibilities more difficult because I wasn't in the building where the bulk of the repairs were needed. Over a five month period I managed to get through it all and finished my Masters Program.

To complete the requirements for my degree, I had to turn in a portfolio containing all the work I'd done during the program, a type of thesis. Dr. Villegas was my advisor. He had observed my student teaching and would grade my portfolio, a very thick binder the size of a large phone book. After my work had been assessed, he loaned it to another student because it was very well done and eye-catching. Somehow, in this student's possession the thing disappeared. Villegas was apologetic. I was livid. That book had all my original, graded work, and represented hundreds of hours of work. After waiting a few weeks, allowing him time to recover the portfolio, I went to the department head and told her that this was unacceptable. Another week went by and it magically reappeared. I'll never know where it went and what kind of plagiarism occurred in its absence, but it was a relief to get it back.

After graduation in December, it was time to go back to teaching classes in January. I was operating under the assumption that I would go back to my computer lab, but my boss told me that she and the vice principal were going to have to interview me if I wanted to return to the school. I originally agreed and then I thought, if she, the woman who has been my boss for five years, wants to interview me, she doesn't want me to work there anymore. So I declined the interview and hit the pavement.

I found a job quickly at a school even further north and closer to my apartment. For most of my CPS career I was living in Evanston against CPS policy, due to residency restrictions for CPS teachers. I have no regrets about doing that, it was quite common and there were plenty of teachers who had been grandfathered in before the rule changed, so they could live wherever they wanted, I felt I deserved the same leniency.

Finding a school so close to my home was wonderful. It was always important to me to avoid a long commute. After completing the school year at my second school, and after summer break, I returned to find that my position was being eliminated and, because I had resigned to do my student teaching, I had lost my seniority and was going to be displaced by a teacher with very little teaching experience. That really blew my mind.

In September of 2002, when I was forced to resign to do student teaching, I contacted a reporter at the *Chicago Tribune* who covered bilingual education and Latino issues. She went to my school to interview me about the injustice of being forced to resign after five years in the classroom, while trying to service an underserved population of students. She published an article about me and other bilingual teachers like me. For years I had heard CPS complain about the shortage of highly qualified teachers, when I did what they required I lost my job. Destiny was telling me to take a different path with my life.

Mazatlán

In March of 2003 I had barely been working at Universidad Americana for two months when something serendipitous happened. There was a textbook convention being held in Mazatlán, Sinaloa, up north. Logic would say that there was no possibility that I would be the one sent there to represent the University's Foreign Language Department. It turned out that none of the dozen, or so, teachers who had seniority over me wanted to go. I got free airfare from Mexico City, but had to pay for a bus to the airport. No matter, I wasn't going to miss the chance.

The flight made a connection in Guadalajara, but there was a mechanical problem with the connecting airplane so all of the passengers going on to Mazatlán had to take a bus for the last leg of the trip. I had already traveled five hours by bus to Mexico City, another five or six hours wouldn't hurt me.

The convention was boring, but I met some nice people. One of them was a woman who I liked a lot, but she was engaged. She said she wanted to introduce me to her sister Denisse. Since I thought this girl was stunning, I readily agreed to meet her. Denisse was an attractive girl who spoke English very well and wanted to be a teacher, like her mother. We hit it off immediately and began a relationship that would bring me back to Mazatlán a few months later.

Mazatlán is an interesting place. There is a small strip of bars, discos and nightclubs, all within walking distance of each other. For some strange reason, although the streets were lined with food vendor carts, the only thing the vendors sold was hot dogs. No tacos, just hot dogs. The night before I was leaving, after hanging at one of the places Denisse liked most, we ate a few dogs and went home, my home being a hotel room. Since she and I wanted more time together we agreed I'd go back as soon as I could.

I went back three months later and we went to the same local nightspots. During the daytime it was imperative for me to find a place to watch the Cubs. They were playing the New York Yankees at Wrigley Field for the first time in decades and I couldn't miss those games. We managed to find a bar that wasn't technically open, but would allow us to spend three afternoons there. The Cubs won the series, making the experience that much better. I met Denisse's whole family. We went to a beach that looked out on the Baja California peninsula with her sister, niece, and future brother-in-law.

Denisse was a nice girl, but seemed kind of aloof at times. When I was back in Acapulco we chatted online daily. I don't know what bug I got in my head, but when she would take a long time to reply, probably due to slow connection speeds, I would think she was playing around, possibly involved in multiple simultaneous chats. While chatting one day, we had a stupid misunderstanding. I thought Denisse was pretending to be her sister to see how I would act while chatting with her. I was wrong, I was paranoid, I ruined the whole relationship. I don't know what got into me.

I had lived in Acapulco for four months and found no girlfriend, then I went to Mazatlán and found one in one day. Long distance relationships are usually a waste of time so when this one ended a few months later, it was for the best.

Sex in Public

I spent dozens of Friday and Saturday nights at La Crissis, my friend Miguel's bar, located almost directly behind Diana la Cazadora. One Friday night I was hanging out, enjoying the live band, and started talking to a tourist from Mexico City. *Defeños*, (people from Mexico City), go to Acapulco by the thousands for long weekends year round. We talked, and drank. I liked her a lot. She was just the type of woman I like and we started to make out. My hands started to wander. We talked of leaving to go to my place. I was ready. She was ready. She said she was with a friend and couldn't leave her. I said, leave her. She said no. While this talk was going on, things got quite hot between us. We were in my friend's bar. There was a small crowd, but it was late. At some point Miguel moved us to the back room. By back room I mean the room that was divided by two steps and was accessible through wide open portals, with no doors. It was 75% as large as the whole bar and was minimally secluded, at best.

I made the best of my time with her there. My hand reached places normally reserved for the second or third date. I continued to invite her to my apartment, she continued to say she shouldn't leave her friend. I felt pretty certain that if things were going so well now, they would go well tomorrow, or whenever she was available. I never saw or heard from her again, although contact was quite intimate that night and all signs pointed to us getting together at least once more.

My friends, especially Miguel, didn't let me forget the lewd acts I engaged in that night. I lived in Acapulco about eight years, for me casual sex was rare, so this was a welcome adventure, albeit somewhat unsatisfying.

Miguel, Miguel, Me, & Yó M.C. Youalli G.

Accosted By a Cop

One night I was hanging out by Paco's taco cart. During the course of the evening we would take turns walking 50 feet down the sidewalk to smoke pot away from the diners and foot traffic, in a little sheltered area next to some restaurants. I went to partake and suddenly I was surrounded by police. Among them was a cop who I knew vaguely, she often cruised by that corner. They put me in the back of their pickup and started to take me in. They may have just been doing their job, arresting a white boy who committed a minor infraction. I don't think so. I pleaded my case as best I could. I explained that I had taught Mexican students in Chicago, I did all I could for the Mexican community. I was teaching Mexicans English there in Acapulco, anything that occurred to me, I said it. Bottom line, I was not harming anyone in any major way. They didn't care, they were taking me in. As we slowly made our way toward their kiosk, the woman distinctly implied that the matter could be resolved if we went to a hotel and took care of business. I wasn't attracted to her in the least. After some tense moments as she continued to try to pressure me, she realized that it wasn't happening. They let me out over by their kiosk which was about two blocks from Paco's *carrito*. No sex. No money. No danger. No problem. This certainly could have turned out much worse. I was probably in much more danger than I thought I was, once again.

Solo Viaje South

After leaving Acapulco in poverty and near desperation in August of 2005, working my ass off for two years to pay my debts, getting diagnosed with prostate cancer and having my prostate removed, (I miss you, buddy!), losing my mother and gaining financial freedom, I decided to move back to Acapulco. I wasn't rich, but I was stable enough to live in Acapulco at my leisure.

My friend John Igliori and his family were living in Texas, so I planned to stay a night there on my way down. I had three cats at the time, Hamlet, Chivo and Squeaky, so arrangements had to be made for them during my visit. I was much more confident about driving down on my own at this point, which meant no frantic search for someone to accompany me. And I was well aware of the driving restrictions in Mexico City, so I had confirmed the days that license plates that ended as mine did could and couldn't drive.

Since the late 1990s, Mexico City has enacted restrictions on which vehicles can circulate on which days, determined by the last digit or number of your license plate. For example, plates ending in "0" or "1" can't be driven on Mondays, those ending in "2" or "3", can't be driven on Tuesdays, and so on. I was concerned that I might not make it on the day I had planned, so I gave myself a cushion, I wouldn't let that issue affect my trip this time. Or would I?

I spent one night at the Igliori's, then drove on to San Luis Potosi and stayed at a hotel where a friend of a friend worked. A girl I knew in Acapulco knew a guy who managed a hotel there, José Luis, and she put me in touch with him.

All went smoothly, although my cats did have to spend the night in a broom closet.

I had no mechanical issues, I had enough money for gas, I knew the traffic circulation rules for Mexico City. All was well. Then I got to Mexico City. The traffic was awful. It was slow going. I had my new GPS, so that gave me some comfort. As I made my way through the city, I was pulled over by a cop on a motorcycle. In Mexico they have about a half dozen different types of police. This one was not a transit, (traffic), cop, so he had no authority to stop vehicles. But I was ignorant of this fact, and probably wouldn't have said anything about it even if I had known.

He may not have been a transit cop, but he knew the traffic rules. He informed me that temporary permits, such as the one I had for importation of my car, were restricted from driving privileges all weekend long. This was a Friday so I was prohibited from driving. He threatened to take my car. I had my three cats and about a half dozen pieces of stereo equipment, a laptop computer and a lot of my other most important possessions. I was in peril once again. The guy seemed to smell the money I had on me. We haggled a little and he finally, *graciously*, accepted about 3,000 pesos, ($300.00) and agreed to escort me to the city border where I would be free of the restrictions. He gave me his name and badge number on a tiny scrap of paper, supposedly as proof he was legit. Then, as soon as I got back in my car to follow him, he took off and I was on my own again.

I had gone no more than a quarter mile when I got pulled over again. These cops explained to me that the other guy was not authorized to issue tickets for traffic violations. On the positive side, this pair was compassionate in their extortion and, when I gave them the 1,000 pesos they demanded, they promised to escort me to the border. They followed through and took me there. It was a challenge because we had to take back roads. When they finally left me to my own devices I was at the city limit, but pretty lost. I drove for nearly two hours until I finally reached Cuernavaca, normally a 45 minute trip, and found my way back to the main highway. It was a nightmare.

Brink of Incarceration

On October 12, 2003 I met Ada Lilia Delgado. She worked as a salesperson person at a well regarded department store in Acapulco, Fabricas de Francia. I saw her sitting on a bench in the mall outside the store. I sat down and talked to her and she accepted my invitation to lunch. We began to see each other for lunch every day. We went to play Frisbee one night on the beach. I spent my birthday with her ten days after we met. She was cute and had a sexy voice. I thought she was going to be my first Acapulcan girlfriend. We went to Carlos Varela's dad's restaurant, known locally as "El Campanario II". Carlos made us some delicious steaks, we had a nice evening. No charge for the meal. Ada Lilia and I kissed in my car before I dropped her off.

On our second date we went to the anniversary bash of B&B, a nightclub situated right over Acapulco bay, on the west end. The day before we went out, I had gone to 105.5, "Extasis", a radio station, where Paco Muñoz was an afternoon DJ. I was kind of a guest DJ. During the time I was there the owners of B&B came by to do on air promotions of the next night's event at their club. As we talked they invited me. The next night I picked up Ada Lilia and took her to B&B. The club was awful, bad music and terrible service, but we made the best of it and managed to have fun.

While my relationship with Ada Lilia was in its initial stages I was also getting to know a girl named Veronica. I met her at a mall too. I was doing my best to make friends and get my romantic life going at the same time.

I taught with Arturo Corona at Universidad Americana de Acapulco. He and I were developing a friendship. He was one of few teachers I spent time with outside school on an individual basis. One day I went to his house in the Pancho Villa neighborhood, which, although not very geographically distant from my apartment, was a challenge to get to. After walking about a mile to a bus stop, I had to go up the mountain in a microbus and then transfer to a regular bus. After the bus ride there was a long, steep, rocky climb up rough ground, and a precarious staircase, to his place.

That afternoon I met his wife, who, it turned out, was a co-worker of Veronica's. Through the course of the afternoon and evening I talked about Ada Lilia and Veronica. A day later, upon returning to work, his wife decided she'd better tell Veronica that I had a girlfriend. For the immediate future this woman ruined my relationship with Veronica, although we remain friends to this day. It is funny how rampant gossip was there, and how it always seemed to revolve around me and women with whom I was often never actually involved, or with whom I had just a few dates.

Another day Ada Lilia and I went to a movie called "Nicotina". After the movie we got a little physical in what would later be the scene of the crime. We were in the front seat of my car, on a dark street, about two blocks from Fabricas de Francia. Although space was cramped, we had a few passionate moments. I was living with Señora Silvia and Humberto at the time, so I didn't want to take her to my place. In order to enter my apartment we would have had to walk through their living room. It was always an uncomfortable situation, even when I was alone. Whenever they were not around to see me pass by I was happy.

On Friday, November 7th I was going to bungee jump and Ada Lilia was going to join me. We went to my apartment, (the only time she ever went there), for her to borrow some shorts from me. She tried on two or three and said they were all unacceptable, so she wouldn't be jumping. She was wearing a skirt for work that wouldn't have been appropriate for the jump. I had told a few of my university students that I was going to do it and was expecting some of them to be there. Only Barbara and her boyfriend arrived. She was taking film classes and had agreed to videotape me. I chickened out. The four of us went for some ice cream. Afterwards each couple went its separate way.

At about 11:00 p.m. I took Ada Lilia to catch a taxi to her house, which is in *La Zapata*, on the outskirts of town where I didn't like going during the day, and never went at night. Before she left we started to talk in the car. I remember clearly wanting not to do what we eventually started to do, make out. I didn't feel comfortable doing it there. Nevertheless, things got hot.

The next thing we knew there were cops around the car. I knew them, they were cops who scored coke for my friend Paco and who hung out at his taco stand, certainly not upstanding citizens in their own right. I told them I knew them, certainly they recognized me. They said it didn't matter now. They started asking me what we were doing, basically saying, "you were having sex, weren't you". I had to get out of the car and, although I knew I was in trouble, I couldn't contain my excitement, I was standing up in more ways than one. They said they were going to take me to Immigration or to the Federal Police. One of them got in my car and started talking to Ada Lilia. He searched my car. He found about a gram of bud. I thought I was in serious trouble. Ada Lilia was extremely upset, she said her ex-husband used drugs and had treated her *extremely* harshly, so she has a very negative opinion of marijuana. Now, not only were we in a fucked up situation with the police, but she was angry because she realized that I smoked marijuana. One disaster at a time was not enough.

The cops kept telling me I was in deep shit and saying they wanted more and more money. I told them I would withdraw all the money I had from my bank account and give it to them. I thought I had close to 1700 pesos there, (about $160). We drove to an ATM to take out the money. One of the cops got in my car with us and he and Ada Lilia got in the back seat. We drove two minutes to the bank. While we were driving Ada Lilia grabbed my video camera and threw it, hard, against the side of the back seat, under the window. It was a tense situation and she was making it worse. While they all waited, I went in to try to get money. I kept trying smaller and smaller amounts. It turned out my balance was only 370 pesos, (about $35). I took 300 pesos because money was only available in increments of 100. I gave the cop the money and he started lecturing me, saying that I should have told her that I smoked pot. I wasn't in the mood for his advice. He gave me back what they had found and he and his partner left. I was lucky that I didn't have as much money available as I thought, they didn't insist on more once I gave them what I had been able to withdraw.

When I got back in the car Ada Lilia started telling me that they had taken 200 pesos from her and the cop had put his hand up her skirt. He had taken her watch and rings and said she had a date with him which she was obligated to keep or he would make her regret not having complied. He implied he would rape her or get her fired, or both. She left without any mention of the camera. Arriving home I noticed that my sunglasses were missing, as well.

After the cops left I vaguely recollect reaching under my seat and touching the camera. I said to myself, "they didn't find it". Did I actually touch it? I can't be certain. When I told Ada Lilia it was missing, she told me not to report it because she was scared they would rape her. She begged me not to report it.

She came to see me Monday at the university and implored me not to say anything, she was scared for her job and her safety. She told me to give her three days to try to get the camera back. She explained that a co-worker had been fired for being involved in something similar. I, being quite naïve, decided to follow her request. She also told me that one of the cops had already called her and threatened her at her job. I believed every word, I was going to wait.

On Monday night I talked with some friends. They convinced me to talk to the authorities. On Tuesday afternoon I went to the American Consulate. The consul sent me to the Tourist Public Defender. I began the process of accusing the policemen involved. José Luis, was immediately summoned to the Public Defender's office with his boss.

These men told us that Javier, the other cop, had not reported for work. I learned Tuesday night that he and José Luis had already talked to my friend and theirs, Paco, and denied fervently that they had taken the camera. In the Public Defender's office, José Luis, who was with me the whole time, said he had never seen a camera and asked me to describe it.

On Wednesday morning Ada Lilia called me and said it was urgent that we meet. When she came to my car outside Fabricas de Francia, she gave me back the camera. She had a neck brace on. She told me she had been beaten, kicked in the head, had severe back injuries, and was on her way to get sick leave at her job and then to get x-rays. She explained how she and her uncle had found the cop, beaten him up, (she said he was a real coward), and recovered the camera. He had sold it but was able to get it back from the person who had bought it.

Whatever it was that happened, she looked fairly good, amazingly good for being a victim in a beating like the one she described. She showed me her watch and said she had gotten it, too. I don't know what happened to my sunglasses or her rings. She informed me that the person who had beaten her up was paying her missed wages and hospital bills.

She also told me she had taken the video tape because she was on it. I have no idea why it was such a concern to her, but, I think it was more of her bullshit. When I tried the camera I found it was broken.

Wednesday afternoon I had a meeting with José Luis, Javier, and the arbitrator from the Tourist Police. Since I had accused the cops of a crime, their jobs were on the line. Unexpectedly, I had the camera in my possession and had no need, or desire, to continue with the complaint. But, justice being what it is in

Mexico, I had to get the cops to agree not to file charges against *me*. At the Tourist Public Defender's office we came to the agreement that everyone would let the matter drop, but because other officials had been apprised of the matter, we would have to discuss the resolution with them before it could all be put behind us.

Everyone at the Public Defender's office who was involved in the case had to go to the main police headquarters, a 15 minute drive away, and talk with Acapulco's Chief of Police. Once we were all installed in the small space, I sat there while one woman told another woman what to write as my statement, absolving the cops of any wrong-doing. She was typing on a 1960s typewriter with a sheet of carbon paper in between the two copies, it was surreal. When the whole matter had been explained to the Chief of Police by me, and the cops, he asked them what they wanted to do about having been wrongly accused, and almost fired, for something that ultimately wasn't true. Although during the arbitration they had agreed to drop all charges, my freedom hung in the balance. If they had said they wanted to file charges against me I would've been officially accused and put in jail. Their delayed response made my stomach drop and I felt I'd be locked up.

After a heart-stopping pause, they said they would not file charges. I almost went to jail for being extorted and having my video camera stolen.

The matter was dropped once we left the police station. Nothing more ever happened between those cops and me, except that José Luis invited me to his house, he wanted me to know that he is not a bad person. He was trying to get me to agree on an amount for them to pay to have me forget the matter. I told him his partner should pay, not him. I rarely saw them after that. On November 18th I talked to Ada Lilia for the third time since everything went down. She said she didn't take the camera. I will never know the truth.

Ironically, over the time I was in Acapulco I had my video camera removed from my possession without my consent twice, basically stolen from me, by Austria and then Ada Lilia, (or the police), and then, when I got a girlfriend I bought her a camera. She was taking a photography class and needed a special camera for it. The video camera I had had so many problems with remained in Acapulco, in my closet, broken, for years before I gave it to a friend.

Ada Lilia and Me

Bye-Bye Video Camera

Austria was the first woman I tried to date in Acapulco. After meeting her while on vacation, I got in touch with her when I moved there. We were developing a friendship and I was helping her learn some English. After knowing her for about two months, she told me about a project she was involved in. Her organization was attempting to bring light to the problem of poverty and poor living conditions in Acapulco, specifically the garbage that was commonly dumped in vacant lots around town. She said they needed to make videos of these health hazards. By making videos they could publicize the problem in an effort to garner donations and community support. This sounded like a worthy cause to me. I wanted to trust her, so I let her talk me into loaning her my cute little video camera for a few days.

When we spoke about her returning the camera to me, she told me she had tickets to the Philharmonic Orchestra that was performing the coming Friday night and wanted to go with me. She would give me the camera that night. When Friday arrived she didn't call me and she didn't answer my calls. I was freaking out. I was not about to let her just walk away with my camera, and it was extra offensive that she had blown me off, too. As I contemplated the situation, I realized that I knew her last name and it was not a common one. Being the amateur sleuth that I am, I deduced that I could take a phone book and find her last name and figure out her address and phone number. She had never given me anything except her cellular number. I called her and surprised her by telling her I knew where she lived and I wanted my camera back. She claimed that she had been sick. I was the one who was sick.

By the time I talked to her it was Monday. Before we hung up I got her to agree to bring me the camera. She finally brought it to me at the university, in between my classes. It seemed to be working fine. It was still in the little bag I kept it in and inside the bag were two tickets to the symphony. Austria tried to make me feel wrong for thinking she wasn't going to return the camera, how could I believe innocent little Austria would take it from me? It was clear she intended to disappear. That was the last time I ever saw her.

Surrounded By Violence

My girlfriend Johana worked at a grocery store called Bodega Aurrera for a few weeks. On June 20th, 2010 I picked her up there at 9:00 p.m. An hour later a man ran in and hid in the employee lounge. Shortly thereafter, two guys showed up, found him, pulled him out and shot him. Afterwards they re-entered and made off with the surveillance video of the store.

There was a prison on the outskirts of Acapulco where Johana occasionally went to buy handicrafts the prisoners made as a way to earn an income. She would then resell them at a profit. One day she was at the prison buying arts & crafts to sell. Suddenly the prisoners she was talking to said all visitors had to leave immediately. Before they could get out there was a lockdown and shooting nearby as some prisoners tried to take control of the prison. At least 50 rounds were fired but no one died.

Murder and Kidnapping for Breakfast

News item from the 30th of May 2010:

Ministerial Police Officer Jesús Gil Navarrete died by gunshot in a confrontation with a group of armed men who kidnapped business owner Joaquín Alonso Piedra when Mr. Piedra exited a tennis court located on Laurel Street in the Lomas del Tigre neighborhood. Regional Ministerial Police Coordinator, Jaime Ramírez Manzanárez, related to the press that, at 9:30 a.m., upon learning of a shooting, he headed to the site immediately and found Officer Navarrete deceased. He spoke with Alfonso Alonso Piedra who informed him that unknown men had kidnapped his brother Joaquín Alonso.

Preliminary investigations revealed that Joaquín Alonso Piedra went to those tennis courts every morning at that time to play tennis. He had agreed to meet Jesús Gil Navarrete there. They had spoken the day before and Gil had asked for a loan, which Piedra agreed to give him the next morning.

The men met at the planned time and were talking in front of the Laurel Condominiums when they were surprised by a number of armed men who began firing on them. Officer Navarrete tried to save the businessman by returning fire. He was assassinated by shots from a machine gun.

The officer's body fell on the front of a parked and locked panel truck nearby.

After the shooting the unknown assailants took control of Joaquín Alonso and forced him into one of the pickups they were driving, leaving Mr. Piedra's pickup on Laurel Street. Officer Enrique Beltrán López and technician Sandra Trujillo Ortiz reviewed the crime scene and found 22 shells from a 7.62 machine gun, 16 from a 9 millimeter pistol, as well as one shell from a 45 caliber pistol.

During the confrontation a Honda CR-V with State of Guerrero plate HEW-4549 that belonged to a neighbor was damaged on its left side.

The remains of Jesús Gil Navarrete, 41 years of age, were claimed by his wife, Silvia Guzmán Hernández. She informed police that she didn't know anything about the events other than that he left home at 9:00 a.m. and did not give a time he expected to return. She requested return of the body so the deceased could be given a Christian burial in the private Paso Limonero Cemetery.

The preceding article is coverage of what happened around the corner from my condominium. The following is my perspective of these events.

I was in my apartment on a typical morning, preparing myself breakfast. I heard some commotion, something that sounded like firecrackers. I was planning to go for a bike ride, so when I finished eating I got ready and headed out to ride down the mountain. When I was about a half block from where the street levels off, I saw that the road below was roped off with yellow crime scene tape. I quickly returned to my apartment.

About two blocks from my condo, where you must turn left to continue down the mountain, there are public tennis courts. At the end of the block, about three blocks from my apartment, some nefarious individuals had confronted a few men who had just finished their game of tennis. One man, a police officer, was killed and another was abducted. A third man remained unharmed at the scene. If I had left home 30 minutes earlier, I might have witnessed it all firsthand.

This was the last time I attempted to ride my bike in Acapulco. Combined with the other violent crimes I saw going on around me, this was enough to deter me from risking life and limb on a leisure ride.

Leaks

Friday the 13th of August 2010 - Diary Entry

As I lay here watching some baseball games, I have to confront the fact that there are some major water issues happening in this apartment. There's a drip that originated about 10 days ago right above my sofa, in the middle of the living room. It is coming from under ceramic tiles on my terrace.

My refrigerator has a problem that began months ago. It leaks a large amount of water from the edge where the door opens. This 'fridge is shit, I've had the part that controls the temperature replaced and it still freezes in the refrigerator part. Levels one and 12, the lowest and highest settings, are both completely unpredictable.

It has rained moderately to heavily for the last 24 hours or so. During that time water came in through the air conditioner in my bedroom. It took a whole bath towel to mop it up. I have a power strip controlling my computer, phone, lamp, and air conditioner there. Luckily nothing was ruined by the water that came in.

In my second bedroom, water came in through the cable TV wire duct creating a puddle of water on the floor, it amounted to about a gallon.

To top this all off, my pool was overflowing because of heavy rain on the terrace. I had to empty and remove it. Because it was situated directly above the leak in my living room, it was likely exacerbating it. So, once again, as I had done many times before, without thinking, I let the air out quickly. The water rushed out and went in the door that leads downstairs to my cats' bedroom. More water than all the other leaks combined flowed rapidly into the room. It took three full towels to mop it up.

My sink faucet has a drip that's been going on for a month, or more, now. Annoying, but not very urgent.

Yesterday my ultrasound confirmed that I do have a hernia, so I have a leak too.

Added to all this, my kitty, Chivo, punched a hole in my screen today chasing a *cuija*, so there's a leak in the screen too.

But, the real irony of the situation is this. For many years now, I have had difficulty starting to pee. With my hernia now, I am having more difficulty than ever, so when it comes to me, I *can't* leak.

On the roof, above my apartment ceiling, water has always been a concern, rain water, to be specific. In Acapulco it is necessary to treat concrete walls with *impermeabilizante*, waterproofing, so they don't allow water to seep through, or become waterlogged. The roof of the property was, by default, my problem. It would be difficult, if not impossible, for me to get my neighbors to cooperate financially if there were roof leaks.

The builder had cut corners repeatedly. The waterproofing he put on the roof was low quality. It rapidly began to peel off, exacerbated by the neighbors who put an inflatable swimming pool on it, trapping water there. Curiously, there was no downspout, just three five-inch square openings in the concrete at the front of the building. This meant that water running off the roof would pour down in torrents onto the cars parked below. The same thing happened when I emptied my swimming pool properly. The water would run down the inclined roof and drench the parking area.

After searching for a while, Inés' dad hooked me up with Silvio, a handyman. He installed a PVC downspout that began at the three openings and ended in one tube. When dirt accumulated near the three openings, the tubes caused a backup on the roof. There was water puddling there for weeks at a time. It started to come in through my kitchen ceiling, right by my front door. Once I realized that it was the downspout that was causing the problem, I had a different one installed and the puddling problem was solved.

When I found someone trustworthy to apply a thorough coat of waterproofing, a small accident occurred. He was working on the east wall of my building and dropped a tool. It fell onto the neighbor's asbestos panel patio roof. I had to go to Home Depot and buy the longest piece of roofing they had. It was not long enough, but luckily my neighbor didn't insist that I get a better one. My convertible Celica made it possible to transport the large, unwieldy sheet with relative ease.

Water

Having been brought up on the edge of Lake Michigan, one of the world's Great Lakes, I had never had the experience of doing without water. Acapulco is a very different story. Not only is it not near an abundant source of fresh water, it is so poor that basic services most people take for granted can be a challenge to obtain. I've already mentioned how hard it was to get light, water, gas and telephone service, but once I had those services, things were far from ideal.

Before I bought my condo, at my first apartment, I had issues with hot water. Looking back it is easy to minimize, or even forget, that I had to take many a shower in very cold water there. I complained quite a bit and eventually the landlord, Don Pépe, came up and checked the situation out. Each time he came to inspect it he got hot water to flow. I continued complaining and we finally determined that I wasn't opening the flow enough, once it was open all the way the hot water did come out. The weeks I endured without knowing this were very uncomfortable.

Bathing in hot water is not a priority for many people in Acapulco. A large percentage of them have no hot water heater, many are accustomed to showering in chilly water when it's wintertime. I never got accustomed to that and showered with warm or hot water even when it was the height of summer. Often, if you shower late enough in the morning, you don't need to use hot water, by 9:00 or 10:00 a.m. the water tank on the roof has had a chance to warm significantly. Generally speaking, though, I used the hot water no matter what time of year it was.

At my second apartment there were drain issues, but I never ran out of water, hot or cold. The bathtub had to be rodded out on more than one occasion because it filled up with shower water when it clogged up.

In many ways, the condominium I bought was a fixer-upper, in spite of the fact that it was in a brand new building. The building's water came from three small *tinacos*, tanks, on top of the roof, actually, above the roof. We were not connected to the sewer system, we had a septic tank under the building. My neighbor, Dolores, always warned of damage to the building if it were not emptied and maintained properly. It was imperative that we get a real sewer connection as soon as we could. There were instances in which the system overflowed into her apartment, a truly disgusting occurrence. After I moved back to Chicago in 2005 I never heard anything more from her about having it emptied or its backing up.

Dolores was on a mission to get us connected to the sewer system from the day she moved in. She was acquaintances with a politician who was charged with maintenance and improvement of city works. Over the years she organized about a half dozen, often impromptu, meetings on our street to discuss our concerns and show this individual and her people the sad situation we were in.

I understood that there was a law which required proper sewer connections on any new construction, but somehow, probably bribes, that regulation was overlooked when our building was built in 2004. Our street was not paved, so we hoped to fix the plumbing while simultaneously paving the street.

The major obstacle with connecting us to the sewer was complicated. Our block is a one block long dead-end street. To enter the street there is a slight upward grade and then, after the apex, a 30 foot decline to the actual street level where houses are built. This made installing pipes a greater challenge than on a typical, flat, street. One idea for connecting us was to run a pipe from our building up to the main road, but that was far from the best approach. That option would require either some kind of pump or having the pipe buried deep enough to avoid the incline. The block is fairly long making this option even more challenging.

Another possibility was to go through the area in front of the neighbor's house at the end of the block. This is essentially the end of the street, there is no car access there, and walking is at your own risk because you pass through that guy's property.

I knew the sister of the owner of that house, but I never knew him. Her nose was very scarred, as if she had had some bad surgery, it must have been violently broken at some point. She spoke some English. She wanted more than friendship with me but I did not. Occasionally she made food for me, and she also asked to borrow money a few times. Eventually she moved away and pretty much disappeared forever, returning only once for a brief time.

Her brother was a nuisance because the only way he disposed of his garbage was by burning it. He would amass a large pile in front of his house then, on a random day, set it aflame. The toxic fumes from all the plastic and other debris were intolerable. If the wind was blowing a certain direction, the smoke would go directly into my kitchen and living room. Burning trash was prohibited, but I would regularly see steady streams of smoke rising from fires around the neighborhood.

It was my understanding that the man living there was a squatter, and working with him was a dubious undertaking. At some point late in the negotiations he agreed to let the city put pipes under his yard, but he was asking an outrageous sum, $60,000.00 or $70,000.00 pesos, (about $6,000). One of the benefits of my moves back to Chicago was that I was not obligated to pay these expenses. There is no condo board in my building, and there is no formal neighborhood committee, so those who are present pay for what needs to be done, and those who are not, don't. We often had to have the street cleared of foliage and other debris, because the grass, trees, and garbage would accumulate and need to be removed. The secluded nature of the street made it a haven for illegal dumping. Many a cab driver would pull into the downward portion of the street to eat, sleep, relieve himself and, sometimes, have sex. It was a little like entering a cave when you drove down that road. The tree in front of our building had hundreds of bats in it, so that, coupled with the seclusion, made it appropriate when I called my driveway the Bat Cave.

The parking area and street had street lights that used expensive bulbs, too, so when they would burn out neighbors would chip in to get replacements. I'm not sure which is better, having specific rules and payments or just winging it, but we did wing it and, largely thanks to my neighbor Dolores, things did get done.

Currently the street is half paved and we are connected to the sewer system. I don't know all the details, though, it was all done after I moved. The worst part is that Dolores has moved away, so what little organization there was is gone.

A huge defect of the block is its width. It is about 20-25 feet wide. This means that it is impossible to make a u-turn in less than a four-point turn. Since it's a dead end street, you either back in, back out, make a difficult u-turn, or pull into the parking area. Our building had one space for each unit. Mine was the furthest from the end which was to my benefit. If there was no one parked in front, I could pull up to the end of the block, put my car in reverse, and back in. Sadly, for most of the time my bad neighbors lived there, they parked in the street. The woman was a novice driver and her skill never improved. She crashed her car three or four times over the years I lived by her. To insert her car between mine and Dolores's in our parking area was nearly impossible for her. We barely had enough room to open car doors wide enough to get out. It was a double edged sword, on the one hand, it was much easier to pull in to my spot if her car was not on the street, on the other, if she did park in her spot, I barely had enough room to get out of my car. If any of us had had an SUV or other large vehicle, it never would've fit in those tiny spaces.

Whenever I got ready to park I had to get out of my car, unlock the padlock on the gate by my parking space, slide the iron door over, and pull in. Another little gift that my second floor neighbors gave me was a severely damaged garage door. Most of the time they lived there they only had one set of keys, so the boy would always climb over the gate to get to the building. This caused the fence to bow in the middle which, in turn, caused it to get off its track and slide only with great difficulty. There were times when I had to put my full weight on the sliding door to get it to move. Eventually Dolores and I paid a guy to fix it. By then the other family was living somewhere else. Now that they've moved back I can only imagine what damage they're doing to the property.

Returning to water matters, on more than one occasion we ran out of it. If you have never run out of water, it can be very hard to fully appreciate how many ways we use it. Of course we need it to drink, flush the toilet, wash ourselves, (hands many times a day), brush teeth, wash dishes, prepare food, clean floors, furniture, etc. The first time you run out of water it is a big shock.

After living without water once or twice you begin to appreciate its worth and, if you are wise, you learn to economize to avoid doing without suddenly.

One time when we ran out multiple days passed without the supply returning. I eventually realized that I had the means to flush my toilet right on my terrace - my pool. Actually, I had to use that water to bathe, too. Trust me, it's much worse to be sweaty and dirty than to clean yourself with water that's been sitting around for a few days and may have some microscopic critters in it. Obviously it wasn't clean enough to drink or use for cooking, but it was *so* nice to have the ability to flush my toilet.

Late in the game I bought a camping shower, but never needed to use it.

I had three different pools up there over the years, but the first one was the best. It was almost three feet deep, had little inflatable, attached seats in two corners, and two cup holders built into each of the sides. The second one was, comparatively speaking, huge. It was about 8-9 feet in diameter and over three feet deep. I had concerns that it would break through the roof because of its weight so I got rid of it. The last one was much smaller and shallower, no more than two feet deep.

Garrafones are five gallon, (19 liter), bottles of water. They are one of the most common drinking water dispensers sold in Mexico. They are very heavy, weighing over 40 pounds. Although they are sold by roaming trucks, as is cooking/heating gas, those trucks almost never went down my street. I did buy water that was delivered to my door on a handful of occasions, but generally I bought *garrafones* at the grocery store and lugged them up to my apartment. This may have something to do with the two hernias I contracted while living in Mexico.

One day I had the good fortune to see a water filter that could be attached to a faucet at Sears, so I bought one. This eliminated the need to buy *garrafones* frequently, but I always kept a few on hand so I'd have drinking water if the city water ran out. When I stopped and reflected on it, I wondered if the filter was actually filtering everything it should, but since I didn't get sick, I have to believe that it did.

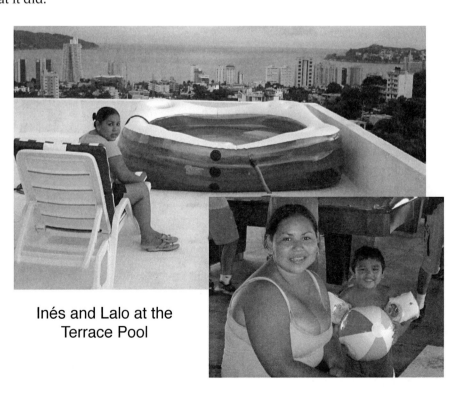

Inés and Lalo at the
Terrace Pool

Discovering Acapulco

The first two times I went to Acapulco were in August of 2002. On my initial visit I stayed at a small place off the main strip, Hotel Magallanes, two blocks from the beach, for just two nights. I had purchased a package deal at the bus station in Mexico City, not wanting to arrive and be unable to find accommodations. Acapulco really wasn't on my radar, but my friends Karla and Hector suggested I check it out. I was visiting them in Mexico City. I decided to go to Acapulco before attending Karla's cousin's wedding in Apatzingan, Michoacan.

After the wedding I went to Zihuatanejo and then back to Acapulco. From Apatzingan I took a bus to Lazaro Cardenas, Michoacan. I had a multi-hour layover before the bus to Zihuatanejo so I ventured out to see the town and have some drinks. I ended up at a bar and fell in like with a waitress named Maria. I invited her to Zihuatanejo and we agreed she'd take a bus to meet me there the next day. I think she was really only humoring me, but I believed her at the time. On the bus to Zihuatanejo I met two women from Acapulco, Marbella and Susana. Marbella had the highest, most girly voice of any woman I've ever met. She was very attractive and dark skinned, a typical woman I like. But she had four kids and she was married. We all stayed at the same hotel in Zihuatanejo.

I spent the evening with my two new friends. The next day they were leaving and, I believed, Maria was arriving. I had to go to the bus depot to meet her. As I waited at the terminal, I saw Marbella and Susana. I had absolutely no explanation for my presence, so I ducked outside and hid until their bus left. Not surprisingly, Maria never arrived. This was to be a recurring theme in my life in Mexico, make dates, go to the arranged meeting point, wait longer than I should, only to be stood up.

In Acapulco I knew no one so the day after I arrived I contacted Marbella. She sent her brother to meet me so he could accompany me to a water park called Los Mochis, near La Barra de Coyuca, about 45 minutes from Acapulco by car. Her brother and I went to the mercado to buy food for an afternoon cookout. We bought shrimp and other seafood. It took us over three and a half hours to get to a place where we should've arrived in about one. Between the buses and the shopping we spent a lot of time, and a lot my money, none of his.

At Los Mochis we met up with Marbella, her children, her sister, and some nieces and nephews. The women prepared the food we had brought and we all ate well. As we ate there was a horde of flies buzzing around and biting us, making the meal unpleasant. While some of us ate others shooed the flies away. They were brutal.

The last time I saw Marbella I ran into her at the last night of Jazz Fest 2009 at the bar Ibiza in the Condesa. She gave me her number, I never called. Four kids. Ain't happenin'.

On this visit I also met Angélica Garcia. Why is that name significant? Because that was my wife's name. Certain names and numbers always come up in my life. The women I date often have the same name or birthday, sometimes both. I did not pick her for her name, she was very attractive to me. She looked a lot like an extra large version of my friend Griselda Ramirez, also Acapulqueña, and she had the same name as my former wife. What couldn't I like about her? Maybe the fact that she never went out with me. I invited her to dinner in the first month I lived there and she turned me down. I called her years later and spoke to her sister. I never did go out with either of them even one time. Why she gave me her number, like about a dozen other Acapulqueñas who never went out with me, I'll never know. I'll never understand that strategy.

Near Drowning

On my second vacation in Acapulco I stayed at the Costa Club, now known as Crowne Plaza. It is located on the beach, but the beach it has access to is not the most accommodating to swimmers. It has a fairly steep incline at water's edge. At certain times of the day it is a dangerous place to swim, as I quickly found out.

I was swimming in Acapulco Bay for the first time in my life and had no idea of the peril I was exposing myself to. I didn't go very far out into the water, but when I tried to get out, I found that I could not. I would get close to the shore and a wave would come and pull me back in. It seemed I was trapped by the lapping waves.

As I struggled to extricate myself from an increasingly frightening situation, I saw that a woman was in the same predicament as me, about 30 feet down the beach. A few people were assisting her to get her footing and get out of the drink. I was not so lucky. No one was helping me, maybe no one noticed how difficult it was for me to come ashore.

It lasted a minute or two, but I was terrified that I would not be able to get out of the water. Attempt after attempt was thwarted by the rushing waves. After a half dozen tries, it finally dawned on me that I could get my footing when the tide went out if I stood up when the water level was at its lowest. As the water receded, although I couldn't get out of it completely, I got to my feet and was standing in two feet of water, easily able to walk out to dry land. I never looked at the ocean in the same way after that. I learned how important it is to be at a flat beach, rather than one that had a steep slope. The waves have far more power than one might imagine. Drownings are common in Santa Lucia, Acapulco's grand bay.

Novias

Inés was my first of two Acapulcan girlfriends. We met one day on Avenida Universidad when I was on my lunch break and she was picking up her son Lalo from pre-school. I invited her to the Fuerte de San Diego and she accepted. While on our date the subject of age inevitably came up. There was a big age difference between us. After exploring the museum we got into my car and were soon locked in a kiss. We began dating exclusively soon thereafter and were together for almost two years. I considered asking her to marry me, but her feelings were not anywhere near as strong as mine. We had lots of fun experiences together and I was treated as part of the family immediately. Her dad had a habit of drinking to excess, so visits to her house were uncomfortable sometimes. He never really worked, so it was hard to respect him as a father. Her mother was a great cook and gave me the royal treatment whenever I dined with them.

A year or so into the relationship we got her a passport and then an appointment with the American Consulate for a visa. We took a bus to Mexico City for the interview and saw a staggering number of people in line there. I did not attend the meeting. Her application was rejected immediately. I had hoped to take her to Chicago to meet my family, especially my father who was gravely ill.

When my financial house of cards began to crumble and I moved back north, she wasn't interested in waiting an indefinite period of time for my return. Our relationship had taken a downward turn when she got a tongue ring. I didn't see the logic in that. When I moved back in 2007 we did not pick up where we had left off.

Inés and Lalo

My only other serious relationship was with Johana, a trained nurse who was working as a waitress at "El Campanario II". I was very intrigued from the first moment I saw her. She was very pretty. I asked Carlos to hook me up and he introduced us. Then when I started to date her he began to act very strange and lied to her about me while telling me stories about her, too. He made me angry enough to terminate our friendship. I had gone for months with no girlfriend and when I found one he tried to sabotage the relationship before it even started.

Johana and I dated for about a year. She had four children whose father was a deadbeat. He caused her no end of worries and offered little financial support. This situation caused discord between her and me regularly. In the end I was glad I moved away because she was much more in love with me than I was with her. She claimed she was waiting for me after I left in 2011, but her declarations of love to another guy on Facebook led me to believe otherwise. She requested that I send her money even when she had another man in her life. Our contact ended on a sour note.

Johana and Me

Harrowing Drive North

The first time I drove back to Chicago from Acapulco I did so because I was deep in debt and about to run out of money, more specifically, the games I played with my debt had created a house of cards that was on the verge of collapse. I owed something in the neighborhood of $50,000.00 and was paying over $500.00 a month in interest alone on my debt. I was earning less than $500.00 a month and was either going to have to run from my financial responsibilities or own up to them. I chose to do the right thing.

I had spent about seven weeks that summer in Chicago working at Truman College, teaching as many classes as I could get while there. I was so broke I didn't even have the $4.00 necessary to ride the "El" train from Evanston to Chicago. I was staying at my mother's house. My dad had died five months earlier. I had my trusty old Schwinn Varsity from the early 80s, so I rode it nine and a half miles each way, one hour's time, to get to school. It was a strange situation. I might have been able to borrow some money from a friend, or my mother, but was reluctant to do so. The fact of the matter was that I was earning the money I'd need to make the drive back to Chicago in August, two months later, although I hadn't faced up to this reality as it unfolded.

Marlene Martinez was a girl I had met at Truman and was interested in dating. One day I ran into her there and got her number. My mother was willing to loan me her car on occasion, so if I got a date I would probably have wheels. I was not letting my finances get me down. I was young and strong and smart and knew that if I worked hard I would always have money. Marlene and I went out once, but when I told her about my dire financial straits she immediately blew me off. I haven't spoken to her since.

A few months later, during the first year I was back working in Chicago, I was so broke I only had money to buy two Whoppers for $2.00 each day, at Burger King, to keep myself nourished, (poorly), during the working week. I was working two jobs and had a total of four different groups of students, so I was running around from morning 'til night every weekday. On Saturdays I worked from 9:00 a.m. until 1:00 p.m. and Monday through Friday I left home by 7:15 a.m. and got home just before 10:00 p.m. Even if I had wanted to grocery shop and make meals for the week, I hardly had time to do so. I was exhausted and my diet and exercise habits were only making things worse. I was tired all the time. I was unaware of the cancer growing in my prostate. It had a negative effect on my strength and stamina, also.

The best route from Acapulco to the border is mostly toll roads. They are very expensive. A one way trip amounts to about $120.00 worth of tolls. The distance from Chicago to Acapulco is about 2,200 miles. Driving my Celica, which gets about 400 miles out of a tank of gas in the best of situations, means I must fill up six times or more. When I moved to Mexico it cost me about $30.00 to fill the tank, so a one way trip ran over $300.00 for tolls and gas, plus two nights at hotels. A one way trip by car cost about as much as a round trip airfare at the time.

As the day of my departure approached I was economizing and calculating the cash I had and would need on the trip. Until then none of the gas stations in Mexico, all state owned and uniform, accepted credit cards, most still do not. Some tolls could be paid with a credit card, but that was never a certainty. If I did not have at least $250 in cash I would not have enough to get across the border.

I managed to scrounge up the cash to make the trip back. I was worried about traveling alone, but had no option for a companion, I would have to make it on my own.

I took my car to my mechanic and asked him to give it a once over so I could be confident that nothing obvious was going to cause me to break down en route. After some searching, we came up with the parts he needed to repair the things he saw that were out of whack. Unfortunately, he did not notice the thing that most needed attention, my brakes.

I had been informed by Karla and Hector that it was best to avoid Mexico City anytime between six a.m. and nine p.m., plus there was the issue of *días de no circula* (days when certain license plates were not permitted to drive in the city). I investigated which days affected my plates and planned to depart at midnight on a Monday, allowing me to reach Mexico City about four a.m. and be out of there by five or six.

The best road from Acapulco to Mexico City is a fairly recently constructed toll road. The quickest route into or out of Acapulco is the Maxitúnel (a tunnel through the side of a mountain that is 295 meters/960 feet, in length). Crossing over the mountain without the tunnel adds 20-30 minutes to the trip.

I got started late, about two a.m. Once I entered the highway I encountered evidence of a landslide, a number of small and medium sized rocks on the roadway. It was dark, there are no street lamps in most areas, and it was raining. I saw a dog crossing the road amongst all the debris. Fortunately, I made it through this natural obstacle course without having any damage or being forced to stop.

As I drove it became evident there was a problem. The brake pedal was reaching the floor. Repairs were urgent. I had no clue where to go so I called Karla and Hector at around 7:00 a.m. I asked for help finding a mechanic. They gave me none. Granted, they had two young boys to deal with, but I thought they might assist me in some way. I found an out of the way parking spot at a gas station and tried to nap while I waited for the work day to begin. When the station opened, an employee guided me to a mechanic. I made it to a shop that seemed safe and was willing to work on my car immediately.

I spent nearly six hours there while they diagnosed the problem and looked for the parts necessary to fix it. They said my brake pads were worn out. By about 4 p.m. they had installed new ones and I was ready to proceed with the drive. Luck was with me because they accepted credit cards.

I managed to make it to San Luis Potosi where José Luis had promised to assist me with my cats again. As was the case previously, I was not allowed to bring the cats into my room, but had to leave them in a broom closet. I didn't like it, but had no other option. They were fine in the morning when I went to get them, my brakes were not. José Luis knew a nearby mechanic and accompanied me over to have my brakes checked again. The mechanic could not determine the problem.

I didn't feel that I had any other option besides driving on. When I got to Nuevo Laredo at the border, the brake pedal once again went all the way to the floor and didn't seem to be stopping the car.

I made it back to Chicago without any major difficulties and immediately took the vehicle to my mechanic. He determined that there was a problem with a broken caliper and it had been seizing up. It was severely damaged due to the fact that it had been catching fire as I drove. I am still shocked by the fact that I did not have complete brake failure or a major fire.

Teaching

When I started teaching at Universidad Americana de Acapulco, (UAA), I was 37 years old and in better shape than I had been in for about a dozen years. I had more than a few admirers among my students and co-workers. For about eight weeks I had a secret admirer who started emailing me. The attention was nice, but it never amounted to anything. It turned out to be a co-worker from the Foreign Language Department who was 18 years old. My admirer didn't inspire anything more in me than a desire to sleep with her, and I didn't want to create an uncomfortable situation at work, so we never went out. I did go out with a girl named Rosy who was a secretary in the office there, but nothing developed from that, either. During my tenure at UAA I never had a physical relationship with any student or employee at the university.

In my first semester, the university gave me three mid-level groups, with a one hour break between one and the other two. This meant that my days began about 10:30 when I walked to work and ended about 3:30 when I got home. 15 hours of work a week, not exactly full time. This was typical for the professors there. Almost all of my co-workers there had another job of some kind, many taught at one or two other schools in addition to the university.

At the UAA there was a prefect who would walk around the halls checking to see that teachers were in their rooms giving instruction. I never saw anything like that at any university I taught at in the U.S. It gave the impression that some teachers would play hooky when they were supposed to be teaching class.

In the Fall of 2003 I was asked to do a seminar at one of the prominent EFL schools, Lang Lab. A co-worker from UAA had spoken highly of my teaching approach to the staff there. I was supposed to show them my innovative style of teaching, which was solidly based around computers. When I went there to discuss the details I saw that they had zero computers, so I decided it was pointless to do a presentation about something they would never be able to implement. I simultaneously decided it was not a good idea to work there because I would not be able to teach in my normal style.

During the time I was at the university foreign language teachers were encouraged to get a national certification from the National Mexican University (Universidad Nacional Autónoma de Mexico, UNAM), so I went ahead and applied. It's always good to have as many documents and certifications as you can get. The exam was divided into three parts, a lengthy essay section, a multiple choice part, and a classroom observation. The first two were administered in Mexico City. The final part was done in one's own classroom. When I got my score for the first two parts it was the highest anyone at my university had ever gotten, 96%. I was a standout among my peers. Then came the practical part where I was observed teaching a class.

I was supposed to be judged by one teacher from my school and one from Mexico City, but it turned out that only the head of the Foreign Language Department and another senior teacher from UAA observed my model lesson. It was a fine lesson with the students collaborating and also videotaping their work. I will forever believe that those women didn't want me to have a high overall score. They graded me very low on the lesson and lowered my final score on the certification. Nevertheless, I was certified and could teach anywhere in Mexico, even today.

In 2004, when I bought my condo, my plan was to teach classes there. On the title I required that it be stipulated that half of the roof was my property, not a common element, as was the other portion of the roof. The building was brand new and the other owners hadn't taken possession yet, so they had not become accustomed to the spectacular view that my terrace affords. As soon as I could get it done, I had a wall put up so they wouldn't be angry that I took away the beautiful view. I struggled to find contractors, (and judging by the awful work that was done on parts of my terrace, I didn't find qualified men), but eventually I got the terrace suitable for classes. The blinding, penetrating sunlight had to be blocked, but there were also some fierce winds that blew every afternoon around five o'clock. After some mishaps with gazebos made of cloth and metal tubing, I had to put a real, cement roof over part of the space. I didn't want to cut off the overhead sunshine entirely.

I had about 35-40 private students during my time in Acapulco, including groups I taught at the Excalibur Hotel. Some of them did study on my terrace, but there were always sun and wind issues, so many of the classes were held in my dining room. The sun is always strong until sunset, with the exception of the short rainy season which prevented studying on the terrace almost entirely.

In the months during which I was still trying to use the terrace for classes, when certain students were scheduled to arrive, I would leave the main gate from the street open. I would also leave the two doors on the roof that led to my terrace open, one gave roof access and the other access to my terrace. At the moment class was scheduled to begin, I would walk up from my apartment and emerge from the inside staircase like a magician through the floor. It still cracks me up to think of it, the only thing missing was a cloud of smoke.

I taught the Secretary of Tourism for the State of Guerrero, Guadalupe Gomez-Maganda. I was contracted to teach her boss, too, but he didn't want a male teacher so that didn't last long. Their offices were at the Centro de Convenciones, which was located on green, expansive grounds, covered with palm trees and formidable hills. There are concerts given there, inside as well as in the garden. It was a beautiful place to work.

The largest and most official private classes I gave were held at the Avalon/Excalibur Hotel. I went in and spoke to a manager there. When I explained my credentials he hired me to teach a group of 15-20 timeshare vendors and support staff four days a week. I had to learn a little bit about the timeshare game before I began. They wanted English classes focusing on the vocabulary and grammar necessary to make sales and close them. I would teach the salesmen the lingo of their trade.

My exposure to the inner workings of a timeshare sale began one morning when I went and observed as the salesmen worked their magic. I shadowed one of them as he ate breakfast with potential buyers and then took them on a tour of the property, before ending up in a room on the top floor where sales were closed. I did not learn the specific details of the process, but my impression was that, once they checked how much credit a couple or family had, they set the price accordingly. It was very strange and, possibly, dishonest.

The room we held class in was at the top of the hotel, it was also the sales closing room. It was kind of scary being up at the top of that building wondering if an earthquake would hit. If there were any temblors during those classes, they weren't strong enough for me to remember. We never evacuated the hotel or anything. It was situated, literally, on the beach. The 20 story structure was the last hotel on the hotel strip before the Papagayo Beach.

Over the months I taught those classes it was quite difficult to get paid. I had to go there multiple times before they came through with the cash. Ultimately, the whole matter was dropped for this reason. I saw some of my students around town for the remainder of my stay in Acapulco, and a few of them studied with me at my apartment for a short period of time.

One of my last students was a plastic surgeon. He lived on the road where Sam's Club was located, farther up the mountain. I would drive to his mountaintop home and teach him for a few hours, twice a week. He told me of giving lectures in English and, every so often, about some outrageous requests for surgery. People would travel long distances to have cheap plastic surgery done. I once translated a long medical paper for him, and he paid me handsomely for it.

My final student was a former secretary from Gomez-Maganda's office, Jackie. She had a new job as coordinator of waste disposal for cruise ships that docked in Acapulco Bay. When the ships would come in, the municipality of Acapulco offered them a comprehensive waste disposal service.

Before I could teach her I had to go and see what her job entailed, similar to the strategy at the Avalon-Excalibur Hotel. She got me special clearance so I could go out on the dock and observe as she interacted with the ship's waste manager. During the two occasions that I went and observed, I saw some frightening things. Massive amounts of garbage, from carpeting to chairs to tables to books to shoes, plus everything else that one might imagine is discarded on a cruise ship. The quantities were astounding. I recall seeing the latest book by a favorite author of mine, John Lescroart, in mint condition, pass by in the mountain of trash as it was shoveled from one receptacle to the next. It was sad, there were a number of items worthy of recovery, but protocol mandated that they all be thrown away. Jackie's company also disposed of liquid waste. Use your imagination.

It didn't take long to realize that my hourly rate was far more than Jackie could afford. I was putting in a bunch of unpaid time and not liking it. Plus, her maritime contacts were from all over the world, couple their myriad accents with Jackie's less than stellar English skills and it was a recipe for disaster. We quickly parted ways.

Bye-Bye Dad

I went to Chicago for Christmas and New Year of 2004. My dad was sick with skin cancer, but was not deemed terminally ill, he seemed to be doing well. Then, suddenly, at the end of January he took a turn for the worse. I needed to go see him as soon as I could. He died hours before my flight left Acapulco for Chicago.

I had bought my condo in August. It took me until early January to find workers to build a stairway from my third bedroom up to my terrace. Until then I was forced to walk out my front door, use the common stairway to the roof, pass through the washing area, and through another door to my enclosed terrace. Having private access was essential. When I learned that my father's condition was deteriorating rapidly, a 5' x 5' hole had already been opened through the ceiling in my third bedroom, and it was imperative that I find a blacksmith/sheet metal worker to put in a door, otherwise anyone climbing from my neighbor's roof to my building would've had free access to my whole apartment. I could not vacate my apartment with it in this state of construction. After waiting a number of days, the guy I had hired finally showed up with my terrace doors. The door for the bathroom did not fit, but he got the main one installed so the apartment was secured. Because of this delay, I was not able to reach my father before he passed away.

When I got back from laying my dad to rest, I was told that the university had no hours for me. They had given my groups to other teachers. The head of the department said I should go to the university's affiliated high school and speak to a contact of hers. I have never taught high school. I never want to. I did not go to speak to the person she sent me to see.

My Dad's Last Birthday, June 2004

Concerts

On a day-to-day basis, Acapulco is somewhat starved for live music. The most common options are cover bands at bars on weekends, and the Philharmonic Symphony which plays two or three times a month during its season. The "Festival Acapulco" was a huge international event for many years, but was reconstituted as "AcaFest" in the early 2000s and has lost steam over the subsequent years. Random beach events focused on music also take place sporadically.

One of my early concert experiences in Acapulco was a Jazz Festival that was held at the Hotel Emporio, which was conveniently located right in front of the La Diana statue. I saw posters about the event in the vicinity a few hours before the final night. Promotion, or lack of it, was always an obstacle when it came time for this annual event.

The night I attended I sat near the front, as I usually do. Through the music I was transported to venues and events that I had rarely recalled in all my time in Acapulco. I felt like I was at the Green Mill in Chicago, the music was so good. Those festivals were always impressive because of the quality of the performers, but there was also a serious flaw in the whole event. Awards were given to all the participants between acts, so after enjoying an hour or so of fine jazz, patrons were obligated to sit through the monotonous, uninspiring reading of the certificates, and presentation of them. If you ever want to suck the air out of a good live show, stop it every hour and read for fifteen minutes. It was difficult to endure, but the acts tended to get better as the night progressed, so it was worth the wait. I had never imagined what exceptionally good jazz musicians there were in Acapulco, and Mexico in general. Although there were non-Mexicans who played these festivals, the vast majority were Mexican. I had never associated Mexicans with jazz. Some of the players were members of the Acapulco Philharmonic Orchestra. They were fine, eclectic musicians, I always wished they had regular gigs somewhere in Acapulco.

The second Jazzfest I went to was also held at the Emporio. This time I was pumped up and ready for the best music Acapulco had to offer. I told all my friends and co-workers that they'd better not miss this event, it was the highlight of live music in Acapulco, not to be missed. I bought tickets as soon as I heard they were on sale, 15 or more. There were three nights and there was a discount for buying all three ahead of the date of the shows. Nefta, Manuel, Chalio, and Marcelo were some of the people who had me get them tickets. I went all three nights from beginning to end, Nefta went to two nights, the others were not as impressed and some did not even stay for one full night, possibly due to different tastes in music.

I recorded all three nights from beginning to end, but gave the original CDs to Nefta and didn't keep copies. I wouldn't have listened to them. He may not have either.

During the entire show one night there was a party going on in another banquet room in the hotel. Their music was very different and very loud. It was almost drowning out our music, significantly interfering with it. During the talking parts of our concerts the other music was clearly audible.

The third Jazzfest I've already written about, it was in the open air at a bar called Ibiza.

The fourth was held at one of the coolest venues I've seen a show at, El Fuerte de San Diego, a military fort built over a century earlier to protect the harbor. The highlight was Rhythm Desperados from the Czech Republic. One of the musicians was so good it seemed he was born with a saxophone in his hands. He was superb. I spoke to him after the show and he told me they were going to New York a few days later. My friend Joe was going to be in New York then too, but unfortunately couldn't attend the show. Rhythm Desperados are definitely a band worth seeing.

The last two festivals were held by different organizations, due to some union issues or something. The Ibiza one was in March and the Fuerte one was in October, since they were not coordinated we got two Jazzfests that year, unfortunately, they were my last.

A few years before this, in 2006, Jaime Virto, took me to a *baile*, to me it was a concert. I expressed my concerns about driving my car into an area where there would be a lot of drinking and rowdiness. He said he'd be able to get me private parking. I ended up driving my car onto the field where the concert was held. I was the only person who drove their car in there, other than the trucks that brought equipment. At this point in time, I would never even consider putting myself in such a conspicuous position, oh how times have changed.

The bands that day played *banda*, basically big band music, each group had about 15-20 members onstage. I don't remember any of the artists by name.

I went to one other *banda* concert at the Convention Center. I started drinking before going. I had some mini bottles of rum and snuck a couple of them into the show. My former student Luis and some of his friends picked me up and we went together. Half a dozen acquaintances were there and some of them were women I liked. Partway through the show I saw Angélica, a girl who I had met many months previously. I liked her a bit. I always felt she was a classy girl who would either be a serious girlfriend of just a friend, but nothing in between. Then at some point she got pregnant without a boyfriend or husband, disproving my theory of her chastity. In my drunken state I decided to open up to her and told her what had always deterred me from making a serious effort to date her. I did guarantee one thing that day, a place in the blundering drunk guys' category, we occasionally saw each other after that, but never went out.

My regular haunts for hearing live music were La Crissis, Zydeco, and Las Yardas. I was friends with all the guys who played there. Two of the most successful artists I met in Acapulco were Yó M.C. Youalli G. and Tony Flynn, they were both friends of Miguel, the manager of La Crissis.

Tony Flynn was world renowned, to a limited degree. He was a guitarist who had played and toured with an incarnation of Steppenwolf of "Born to Be Wild" fame. He also toured as part of a group calling themselves Deep Purple. Rod Evans was the original singer for Deep Purple and he felt he had the right to use the band's name. When he got sued by Ritchie Blackmore and other Deep Purple members and lost, he learned that he was mistaken. Tony, Rod and their band could no longer tour under that name.

Tony was married to an Acapulcan woman. He had been residing there for quite a few years, but would go to northern Mexico during part of the year. I saw him play a few times at La Crissis. Miguel was always trying to get him to play there, but he rarely did.

On one of our Sunday's at El Morro on the beach, Tony was there and someone had an acoustic guitar. We had the distinct pleasure of hearing him play a half dozen songs at the edge of the ocean, on the beach. "Red House", by Jimi Hendrix, was one of the highlights. He talked about his experiences with famous musicians like Eric Clapton and Keith Richards when I asked about them.

Yó M.C. Youalli G. was a native Acapulcan. He was very dark skinned and told me about being treated as a foreigner by local police, evidently due to his complexion and attire. He had long dreadlocks that almost reached his waist. He was a congenial guy who stood out in any setting. He liked to get high. I bought an mp3 CD of his music from him and still enjoy some of the songs. His best songs are, "México Seguro", "Híjole" and "La Indiscreta".

"México Seguro" is about an experience he had when he was walking down the street minding his own business. Unexpectedly and without cause, a bunch of cops stopped him, searched him, and took him to jail. This was one of the times he was discriminated against for being a "foreigner", the cops thought he was Nicaraguan and had no documents to prove his legal status in Mexico.

One of the last times I saw him was at La Crissis. He was living in Mexico City at the time. He asked me for money for his bus fare back. I gave him 250 pesos with the promise I'd be repaid in the coming months. The next time I saw him I reminded him of the loan and he repaid me with his new CD. I was glad to not count him among the long list of people I'd loaned money who never paid me back.

While in Mexico City I had the pleasure of meeting and partying with my friend Hector's cousin's reggae band, Los Rastrillos. His cousin is the drummer. I got to see them play in El Zócalo in Mexico City once. I hoped to arrange a meeting of Yó M.C. Youalli G. and the band, but was never able to do so.

Weddings

My first wedding in Mexico took place in Apatzingan, Michoacan in 2002, when I was on vacation. This was the summer before I moved to Acapulco. Years later I found out that Apatzingan is one of the epicenters of narco-land Mexico. My time there passed without incident.

I met up with Karla and Hector, who drove from Mexico City. Our hotel was very rustic and unique. It had a large open-air patio in the center of the rooms. I travelled from Acapulco, taking three or four buses to get there. The last one was a ride I will never forget. It was a minor miracle that I made all the connections smoothly.

I left Acapulco in the morning and connected through Lazaro-Cardenas. From there I went through Morelia and connected with a direct bus to Apatzingan, a red-eye. It was little more than a school bus. The road to Apatzingan is mountainous and curvy. I was dead tired. As I slept the bus careened from one side of the road to the other, up and down the mountain. My sleep was disturbed time after time as I crashed into the side of the bus or was nearly thrown to the floor.

Over 100 people attended the wedding. I met Karla's family and we participated in the events as family. Hector sang some ballads, I impressed some people with my Spanish. I met Rocio, Karla's cousin. I liked her and we exchanged info and, later, an email or two. I never saw her again, though.

The second wedding I attended in Mexico, my first in Acapulco, happened by chance. I was with Felipe Rico. As I've mentioned, Felipe is a master mooch. He has an ingratiating personality, he seems to mesmerize you. But he's a friend without funds. So, in honor of his presence he allows you to pay for everything. Maybe I'm exaggerating a little, but he has friends everywhere who treat him to drinks, food, and fun.

Felipe and I were driving around, albeit far from where we lived. A convertible in Acapulco is pretty cool and we were putting it to good use. We were about 45 minutes west of Acapulco in the area called *Barra de Coyuca*. We ended up at a venue owned by friends or family of Felipe's, and a wedding was taking place there. We ate, we drank, we had a great time. I danced with at least one woman. We didn't pay anything. I won't say I didn't benefit from Felipe's ways.

My third wedding was friends of Jaime Virto. He was DJing and I was a little out of place by myself while he worked. This one was in Acapulco proper, pretty close to downtown. I have a bunch of pictures from the event. It was a lively event with Jaime laying down the soundtrack. The food was good and the dancing was fun.

The fourth wedding I attended was held in the *Renacimiento* neighborhood which is a place I rarely went and wasn't keen on going to for this, either. Carlos convinced me all would be okay. The parking area had an attendant, which was a small relief. Carlos was the *padrón del brindis* so he had to bring champagne and make a toast. The wedding was very elegant, at least as elegant as a wedding can be at a big box venue with a plain cement floor. They had a nice, large, tiered cake. There were about 200 guests. I met a girl named Iris, who gave me her phone number. I thought there was a good chance we'd go out because we were friends of friends, but I never saw her again. I called her and asked her out, but we never got together.

My final wedding was very close to my condo, about five minutes away. The bride and groom were friends of Nefta's. The wedding had an elegant spread and was held in a typical reception hall and had all the typical matrimonial accouterments. About 100 people attended. I talked with Nefta's mom and some other folks at our table who were old college friends of his. A few months prior to this I had shared a typical Mexican Christmas dinner with Nefta, his mother, and family which made my holiday special.

Funerals

I went to a couple of funerals in Acapulco, too. The first was in 2004 when my girlfriend Inés's grandmother died. It was interesting to see the rituals surrounding death there firsthand. The wake starts almost immediately. The body is kept at home. After 24 hours the body is moved to the graveyard and buried. Things move much more rapidly there than they do in the United States. The immediate family stays with the deceased until the burial.

Ricardo was my co-worker at Universidad Americana. He spoke English better than just about anyone else at the University, with the exception of me and Dolly. I saw him more than once jogging on *Avenida Farallon*, one of the main streets near my house. He was a nice guy, we always exchanged friendly conversation. He had learned his English while living in the U.S. for a few years.

About a year before any of the Fernando stuff went down one of my co-workers from the university contacted me and told me Ricardo had committed suicide. The story was in the news, I had heard about it before that person contacted me, but I didn't know it was my friend.

His wake was held near the *via rápida* and the Social Security hospital. The roads are quite disorganized and congested there, they curve and intersect in unpredictable fashion. I spent a little time at the wake, possibly not as long as most Mexicans normally do. I spoke to Ricardo's mother and told her I had always considered him a friend. I expected to see co-workers there, but did not. There was a mass at a church close to my house a day or two later. I saw four or five co-workers at the service. I hope his decision brought him peace. I wish he were still alive.

The other funeral I attended was Fernando's. It was held close to Icacos, where he had lived. His family's house was relatively close to his apartment. It was a short ways up a mountain. Johana's family and I were all worried that there might be more violence at the wake. I saw people who were rumored to be responsible for his death there. Luckily nothing unexpected happened. Fernando's brother and cousin were friends I had spent some time with before his death. It was hard to see them in such tragic circumstances. I hung out with his cousin once after it was all over and talked to his brother about getting together, but we never did.

Caves

Since I was about ten years old I have been fascinated by caves. I went to the Cave of the Winds near Colorado Springs, Colorado for the first time then and was hooked. I have toured that cave a half dozen times over the years. When I was on my honeymoon I took the special spelunkers tour with Angélica. We had a great time crawling around on the cave floor with flashlights, getting dirty from head to toe.

I was drawn to the caves in Mexico when I learned about the ones in my proximity. The most famous one in Guerrero is near Taxco, which is about three hours from Acapulco by bus. The Grutas de Cacahuamilpa are a big tourist draw. While I was dating Inés I organized and financed a trip for her, her mother, her son Lalo, and myself. There were frequent bus departures from Acapulco to Taxco, so without prior reservations we arrived at the terminal and caught the next bus. I had wanted to leave much earlier, but we ended up leaving quite late.

When we got to Taxco it was already afternoon. In order to get to the caves we would have to travel another 20 minutes on a local bus. The caves closed fairly early, so there was no point in trying to go. We never reached our intended destination, but spent the afternoon walking around the rustic, colonial town. I still haven't visited those caves.

Some months prior to this fiasco, I spent the one and only night I have spent in Chilpancingo, with Inés, at her cousins' house. We were there to visit the much less known, and less touristy, Juxtlahuaca Caves. This time we did actually complete our mission.

These caves were a very underdeveloped tourist destination. As you arrive in the town nearby, you must find a guide by asking the locals where one can be hired. There are people certified to give tours, but they are not well organized. We found one without much difficulty, though.

There are none of the common aspects you find at most caves where novices can tour and explore here. The only lights were the flashlights we took with us. The entrance was a little scary because there was a multitude of bats who lived near the mouth of the cave. This made navigation a little tough, too, because there was a lot of *guano*, (bat feces), on the ground. After a few hundred feet, it tapered off, most of the bats live near the mouth of the cave. We were warned to be cautious of the flying bats that could swoop down and smack you in the head.

Two things stand out most clearly for me about this trip. One was how we had to wade through pools of water as much as four feet deep to access certain parts of the cave. It was unique, exhilarating, and a little challenging. The other, sad, part of the trip is the fact that, in spite of being obsessive about backing up all my hard drives at least once, I have lost the pictures we took there. I have reason to believe they may be on a damaged hard drive of mine, but I cannot get data off of it unless I pay someone $500 to recover it. Someday I may do so.

Puerto Escondido, Oaxaca

Disc golf is a game I have loved since I was 13 years old when I first played the course in Wilmette, Illinois. Since then, I have made an effort to play it whenever and wherever I can. When I read online that there was a disc golf course in Puerto Escondido, I set about planning to go. Puerto Escondido was seven hours away by bus. I was still friends with Felipe Rico at the time. He told me his cousin was a well known doctor there and that he had a kind of hotel I could stay at. Things were falling into place.

I was working at the university and had to wait for my vacation. I would travel during Easter week, thus avoiding the overwhelming crowds that converge in Acapulco around that time.

Felipe gave me his cousin's phone number. He suggested I just arrive and ask the cab driver to take me to Dr. Pépe's. I was assured that, due to Puerto Escondido's relatively small size, and Dr. Pépe's notoriety, anyone I asked would know where to go.

The bus ride between the two cities lasts as long as it does because of the copious number of *topes*, speed bumps, between Acapulco and there. There are about 700 of them. A driver that disobeys the speed bumps will ruin his vehicle's suspension and may do it other severe damage. They are infallible, except when the locals manually remove them, which has been known to happen often.

I arrived at 8:00 a.m. after an overnight ride and the first taxi driver I asked said he knew where Dr. Pépe's was, so he took me to the doctor's complex about two miles from the terminal. It turned out that the good doctor was a gynecologist. I was told he is known for treating the prostitutes of the city. There were women waiting in his outer office, but they could've been anyone, of course.

The doctor was one of the founding fathers of modern Puerto Escondido and his property reflected this. It is situated on a large hill overlooking the main beach and bay. I never got a clear idea of exactly how big it was, but it had at least a dozen guest rooms and enough space for the medical practice.

The first time I stayed there I had little contact with the doctor, but what contact I did have was very pleasant, he was a friendly guy. He didn't charge me a cent for my room and it was quite possibly the most spacious in the building, albeit still under construction at the time. It had a very large, open-air terrace, with a palapa ceiling, overlooking the beach. There were two or three bedrooms in the main living space, as well. This was a luxury suite.

I headed over to the beach to inquire about the disc golf course. Online I had read that the owner of an oceanfront restaurant was the person I needed to see, so I found his restaurant and told him why I was there. He was a great guy with a cool restaurant, unfortunately, I have no recollection of his name. He was an American ex-pat and a partier who welcomed me to the fat spliff he kept in the bathroom at all times. But my luck was to end there. The disc golf course was no course at all, golfers just threw at selected objects along the beach. Since it was Easter week, the beach was quite full and no games could be played. It was a big disappointment.

I found myself on one of the most pristine, exquisite beaches I had ever visited, so disc golf was easy to forget. I did notice a not insignificant amount of garbage littering the beach and it didn't take much longer to realize that much of the problem stemmed from the lack of garbage receptacles in the area. Whether the people wanted to throw their trash away or not, there wasn't anywhere to put it if they did. I decided to spend some time cleaning up the beach.

An eye-catching, unique, rocky outcropping divided the beach in two. It was low enough so that everyone could climb across, approximately 30 feet high and 30 feet wide, so the incline was not steep. There were enough different groups of rocks that the cracks and plateaus that joined them were prime locations to stash trash.

Over the years I have come to accept the fact that a large portion of Mexican people seem to be oblivious to the ugliness and unsanitary conditions created by throwing garbage anywhere and everywhere. Many a Mexican national has told me it is part of their culture. It is something I detest.

I was ceaselessly reminded of this attitude in Acapulco. One time I was on a *camellón* that divided the traffic in Acapulco in front of the mall, Galerías. Some high school kids were stranded there with me, waiting for traffic to let up. They threw some large pieces of trash on the ground and I confronted them. I asked them if they lived in Acapulco and they said yes. I told them it was sad to me that I, an American, not Acapulcan, would care about their city more than they did. In a city often referred to as paradise, it was particularly offensive to litter the street with garbage.

In Puerto Escondido, as I collected the mess, I struggled to find bags to put the stuff into. I asked at a restaurant, which virtually straddled the same rock formation, for some bags. They gave me a few large ones. I know I looked strange, this chunky, tall white boy, walking along and cleaning the beach, but I hope I made an impression, maybe some of those people who saw me doing that adopted a similar attitude after seeing me.

Puerto Escondido is quite a small town with little to do at night. While talking with locals, I learned of a rave happening a ways up the beach. When it got dark I joined some other people who were going there and walked to the gig which turned out to be a wild, rockin' bash. There was a ton of beer, a little bit of bud, and about 100 people. A large tent had been set up and there was another, more permanent, enclosure, but most of the people were on the beach by the bonfire. Some kids were spinning nunchucks and dancing, one even kept them flaming as he swirled and maneuvered around.

What made that night even more amazing was a person I saw. Zihuatanejo is in Guerrero, eight or ten hours north by bus. I had been there three times. The last time was about six months earlier. Unexpectedly, I ran into a girl who I had met there on my last visit. Talk about a small world.

Since I could not play disc golf, I tried to do the next best thing, play Ultimate Frisbee, a sport not unlike American football or Mexican futból. You play with teams and goals like futból and throw the Frisbee from one teammate to the next, the player with the disc cannot move his/her feet. On the beach I saw a group of four girls who I wanted to meet so I asked them to play with me. We got two teams together and played for a while. It was a blast.

After that I talked them into going up to see my hotel room. We were almost directly in front of my hotel/Dr. Pépe's house and I had a gigantic, glorious open air terrace that was not meant to be enjoyed alone. They came up and we hung out for a while. I kept in touch with one of them for a year after that, but don't even remember any of their names now.

My other trip to Puerto Escondido was also a mission to play disc golf. Once again my quest would be thwarted. I had arranged with Dr. Pépe to stay at his place again. When I arrived I found that the suite of rooms I had stayed in alone the last time was now being occupied by an American and his Oaxacan girlfriend. His name was Jim, hers escapes me. I would still stay in the suite, but would only have one of the bedrooms. No big deal.

Jim was one of the short succession of Americans I met in Mexico who seemed to be running from the law. Financial chicanery comes to mind when I think of him. I never was clear about what his deal was. He had severely injured his foot and this little woman, who, coincidentally, was a nurse, took him under her wing. She worked for Dr. Pépe. They were now a couple, he in his 50s, she in her late 20s. I got a negative vibe from the guy, but he was alright to hang out and party with, and I didn't have much choice because we were in the same suite.

One day Jim, the nurse, Dr. Pépe, and I went to a farm Pépe had in another part of town. He had some interesting wooden sculptures and a lot of farm animals there. We spent time on the water. Dr. Pépe had a kayak which the four of us took turns using. Dr. Pépe and I took it a short ways to another small beach. I was terrified we were going to tip over and ruin my brand new digital camera. I had never been in a kayak before. No capsize occurred. Later the four of us had dinner at a nearby restaurant.

In my investigations about where disc golf was being played I found that the guy who organized it had moved to another part of town. He was the same American ex-pat I met on my first visit. I got a cab and went over to his new restaurant. He informed me that he wasn't playing much those days. For a while games had been organized in another area, but no one was playing anymore. So, disc golf in Puerto Escondido was essentially a thing of the past.

I sought out a rave more actively and heard a rumor that there would be one that night. The town is pretty dull if you don't make your own fun, it closes down very early. As night fell I found myself hanging with a trio from Puebla, two guys and a girl. They were pretty young, but since everyone can drink in Mexico, the age difference didn't seem as pronounced. They were living in Puerto for a short period of time, but were almost out of money, so they would depart soon. I liked the girl and she liked me, soon we found ourselves intertwined on a park bench making out. It quickly became obvious that she had taken Ecstasy. One of my most vivid recollections of the trip was the moment we were kissing and she could not control her jaw. She was like a piranha, I couldn't kiss a woman who was primed to bite my tongue off. I subtly ended the kissing and hugging and got everyone on the road to the rave.

The event was much farther down the beach. We walked, and walked, and walked. It seemed that the rumor had been false. We walked nearly two miles. When we finally made it to the location, it was well into the a.m. and the party was dwindling. The vibe was much less fun than the first one. We didn't stay too long.

Before I departed I saw Dr. Pépe. He accepted payment for my accommodations, but only charged me $20 a day for a room right on the beach, I was happy to oblige.

Terrace at Dr. Pépe's

Baseball and Auto Racing

While on vacation in Mexico City before I first visited Acapulco, I went to a professional baseball game. The local team was the "Diablos". I was with Hector and his cousins, there were six or seven of us. The opportunity to see a good baseball game in a foreign country is something I don't pass up. We had our fair share of beers over the nine innings, we passed a joint or two, also. The game was good and we sat about 20 rows in back of home plate.

After the game was when the fun really started. This baseball diamond, Foro Sol, was built in the middle of an auto race track, the Autódromo Hermanos Rodríguez. I didn't realize this until after the game. When we left it was dark and many patrons had vacated the stadium area. We went to our car, a late model Volkswagen, and proceeded to head toward what we thought was the exit. Shortly thereafter we realized that we were driving on the race track itself. The road twisted and turned as we drove along looking for the exit. It became evident that, not only were we among few cars still remaining, but there were no monitors or guards of any kind. We started to race around the unlit track. The swerves and curves flung us and our vehicle from side to side, we were on a professional race course with no one to tell us what we could or couldn't do. It was thrilling, as long as we avoided the curbs, we wouldn't crack up.

Upon reflection, I, once again, feel incredibly fortunate that the night didn't end in disaster. There were no lights other than our own, so the hairpin turns came unexpectedly, but by the time it was over I was ready for more. I was screaming "vuelta, vuelta", (another lap, another lap), but, sensibly, we took the exit and the checkered flag came down.

Work Visa

In January of 2003 I was hired at the Universidad Americana de Acapulco where I had interviewed the previous August while on vacation. They explained to me that getting a work visa would not be difficult once I had a job and could prove my expertise and education with proper documentation. They gave me a letter stating that the university wanted to hire me as a foreign language professor.

After class my first day, I went to the Office of Immigration where visas are granted and general governmental documentation is obtained. In Mexico paperwork is king. Nothing is true until you have a piece of paper that says it is so. I had brought my original, framed diplomas to Acapulco, thinking that they would be sufficient. They were not. I was obligated to provide officially certified, notarized copies, (*apostillados*), of my transcripts before my visa would be granted. Luckily I did not have to stop working while procuring my documents. I contacted Loyola University and Northeastern Illinois University and had them issue official transcripts which then had to be officially notarized before being sent to me in Mexico. It was a complicated, lengthy process.

Over the course of a month, I managed to get the papers sent to me with the official seals immigration wanted. It was costly. The visa itself cost me more than $150. I was hired at about 100 pesos an hour, ($10.00 at the time), but after taxes were taken out I made about $8.50 an hour. Just getting my documentation in order cost me two full weeks' pay.

In 2003 the immigration office was very poorly organized, you never knew when you would be attended to and it appeared that it was pure luck if you were attended to in the order you arrived. Although it was only a few miles from my apartment, I had to walk down the mountain to catch the bus unless I wanted to spend money on a taxi. A trip to deal with my visa generally took three hours or more. Waiting in line is common in Mexico and the immigration office is no exception.

When I finally got everything in order with my docs, I had to find a way to receive my salary, to have it deposited into my account. There was an HSBC bank exactly in front of the university and teachers were given special, low fee, account options. I naturally decided to bank there. The pittance I earned was deposited automatically.

Twice a month I had to go to the accounting office of the university to sign my payroll paperwork. It was very strange. This was another bizarre time consuming activity necessary to receive my pay. All the accounting of hours worked and income earned was done manually. It was similar to going to pick up a paycheck, but all the documents I had to sign, with multi-use carbon paper between the pages, seemed archaic. So much rigamarole to receive a paycheck that never amounted to more than a few hundred dollars for a half-month's work.

The HSBC I banked at had a strange time-lock door that only let 3-4 people enter or leave at once. If you were going in you often had to wait in a line on the stairway while people passed through the double door with a chamber in between. This system was fraught with dangers, although it was fairly secure from a bank robbery perspective. From a patron's, or employee's, perspective it was truly a dangerous proposition. Acapulco is situated on a fault and has frequent earthquakes. If that bank building were to have suffered a strong earthquake, everyone inside could have been trapped. Recently the bank was remodeled and the chamber doors are no more.

Fiesta Time

Over the years since I graduated from college I have hosted about a dozen parties and each time I have one I say it will be my last. I had a half dozen of them over eight years in Acapulco. Usually less than half the people I invite come, but those who do generally have a stimulating evening. It was difficult to resist sharing the beauty of my terrace in the center of the bay.

One of the earlier ones was held to celebrate the end of the school year. A bunch of the invitees were my university students, Luis, Mario, Eder, and a few more. I had some amicable guys and girls in my level three class. The thing that makes this party stand out in my mind is the way it ended.

It was getting near dawn and Mario was crashed out on a chaise lounge on my terrace. He had drunk a large amount of alcohol and was dead to the world. His ride was leaving, the party was over. We tried to wake him up. When we finally got him awake he freaked out, and started getting angry and aggressive, he was unaware of his surroundings. Punches were thrown, it was a very tense scene while these guys tried to get Mario to understand where he was and what was going on. That was not the only occasion I saw Mario go way over his limit.

My terrace is three flights above ground level. It was a struggle to get this guy downstairs, but Luis and others managed to do so. However, Mario was still in a combative mood. When they got to ground level and out to the jumble of cars parked in the street, Mario put his fist through Carlos's window. Ultimately they got him to go home with no further confrontation. The matter went on for a few weeks while Luis and I coordinated contact between Carlos and Mario so Mario could pay Carlos for the window he broke. Eventually, Mario paid to have the window replaced. Luis told me Mario tried to curtail his drinking after that. I hope he stopped. This was the only party I ever had at which violence occurred.

During the first semester I taught at the university, I attended a party at another teacher's apartment. It seemed most people were there just to kiss the boss's ass. I didn't get a great vibe that night, there was a subtle undertone of formality and tension.

One Sunday night I had an impromptu party with the guys from the band La Riata who were playing at Zydeco. During a break, Pablo, Fer, Pedro, and I drove my beautiful Celica, with the top down, up the mountain to my condo, fired up some bud, and headed back down for them to do another set.

My last party turned into two parties. I planned it for one night and Patricia and some *Universidad* professors came over the day after the real party. There was a mix-up about which night it was to be. I made rum punch for that party. I figured, we're in the tropical heat, the only thing missing is the Caribbean Rum Punch. It was a big hit, both nights. Fernando and Pablo from La Riata came again. We all celebrate birthdays in October. A few days later Pablo had a birthday party and we made the same punch for his guests.

The second night was weird and ended abruptly when my guests decided they were going to go somewhere else to get dinner. First we were talking about ordering in, and the next thing I know they're all leaving. I didn't want to go. The group included Patricia, her husband, one other couple, and a woman I had no interest in who was supposed to be my date.

Informal family get-togethers occurred sporadically, too. On more than one afternoon I had Carlos, his woman Chantal, and their four kids over. The kids always loved to play in my pool up there in the sky, overlooking the bay and the neighborhood, it's pretty cool to be in a pool.

Johana, her three kids, her sister, niece, and nephew enjoyed some afternoons in the pool there, too.

I had Ines's family over for dinner one time. She and I made an elaborate dish using a Rick Bayless cookbook I had. I had a few 4th of July parties and even one Thanksgiving party, complete with pizza from Chicago.

Somewhere around 100 people partied on my terrace over the years I lived in Acapulco. How many were my family? Zero. How many were friends from out of town? Two. How many times did I have sex up there? Intentionally left blank... I only slept there overnight when I fell asleep accidentally, maybe three times. It's a little daunting to sleep under the stars.

Johana's Kids, Niece, and Nephew in the Terrace Pool

Struggles with Stereos

I became an audiophile at a very young age. I like to have access to a wide variety of music and my collection is constantly growing. I had a subscription to XM Satellite Radio beginning in about the year 2000. I thought XM would be the future of radio, and in some ways it is. I invested in the company but didn't make too much of a profit in the end, having to sell some of my stock at a bad moment when I was hard up for cash.

When I moved to Mexico I figured I would have to give up my satellite radio, but I discovered it's hard to control a satellite signal within a specific geographical range. My home XM signal never failed me down south, except in heavy rainstorms. I bought the longest extension wire I could and ran it from my XM receiver to the top of the roof over my terrace, the highest point in the building. I wound the wire around the exposed rebar that composed the corners of the structure so the wind could not blow the antenna down. I originally set up six speakers on my terrace, running wires from my living room, along the third bedroom ceiling, up the stairs, and out the door. Two of my speakers were "all weather" so rain didn't damage them. Two others were cheap, old, Aiwa brand that I put in plastic bags during the rainy season.

My intention was always to have control of the music I was playing. I had my iPod, XM Radio, and even the DirectTV audio signal all connected to my stereo receiver. It was important for me to be able to select songs and change sources wherever I was in my apartment. I experimented with remote control senders for the first four or five years. I could point the remote at a sensor that would relay the message to a receiver in front of the stereo receiver. It worked fairly well for a while, I could change between sources as well as change XM stations and iPod songs, but my building's thick concrete walls made it difficult. I bought three different kinds of infra-red (IR) remote control senders over the years, one of which I gave to Carlos because he was enthralled with it. If you have a second floor and only one stereo, it's especially important to have control of the stereo from above. It's one thing to walk into another room to change a song or station, it's another to walk down a spiral staircase and into the next room, especially if you are imbibing and/or relaxing in a swimming pool. Every so often, since I had my TV connected through the receiver, and DirectTV signal from the United States, I would be changing sources and the remote sender would fail. American TV would start blasting from my speakers blanketing the block with some court program or a game show from the 1970s.

As much as I tried to avoid it, more than a few times, my neighbor would get very angry because of the volume of my music. He would throw things like small candies up onto my terrace or at my window to get my attention. His terrace was a full story below mine.

On too many occasions I had battles with the idiot who lived below me. He considered himself a DJ and would practice at all hours. He never played any music other than techno, which I find hard to classify as music at all. He also played his music as loud as he possibly could. It would keep me awake at night and wake me up in the morning. He was always disturbing the neighbor in front like I did. In order to combat his high decibel cacophony, I set up my large floor speakers in my second bedroom directly above his bedroom. I would turn off all the other speakers and crank those up in order to avoid hearing the trash he was pumping out day and night, sometimes until dawn. It was a great day when he moved out and a sad day when he moved back.

After the third IR remote sender became useless, I finally gave up and got a second stereo that I put on top of my terrace refrigerator inside the stairway door. It was much easier to change the music that way, and by then I had long since abandoned my XM account so the only device I listened to up there was my iPod.

As I drove down south and crossed the border for the first time, I believed that as soon as I was on Mexican soil the XM signal in my car would cease. I was pleasantly surprised to find that was not the case. It worked until I was well down into the country, at an area south of San Luis Potosi. Once it stopped I figured that was that. I had always kept the antenna, which resembled a large computer mouse, inside the windshield on the dashboard, I wasn't wise enough to try it outside.

One day I was hanging out at Paco's taco cart and changed the input to XM. Voila! the music played. I took it to mean that I was in a special spot where the signal could be received. I played XM music for all of us as we passed the nights there. I still did not realize that I should take the damn antenna out, though. I also found a spot up on "La Escénica" where there was a parking lot that faced the right direction where I could listen, too.

My car stereo had a removable face plate as an anti-theft precaution. I was negligent in its care. It fell on the ground on occasion. One day it fell and was damaged so the screen was dark. The stereo still worked, but changing inputs and other functions was a challenge.

About the same time I had an epiphany, realizing that I should put the XM antenna on the outside of the windshield. This allowed me to hear satellite radio anytime and anywhere, but the broken face plate made it near impossible to tune in the stations I wanted to hear. I took one step forward and one step back.

On my next trip to Chicago I got a new stereo, it was cost prohibitive to repair the one I had. I brought it back and had a friend of Paco's who had a stereo installation shop install it. As he began to do the work he cut the wires to the XM box which was located under the seat. Inexplicably, reconnecting the wires did not bring back the signal. Once again, I took a step forward and a big step back. Now I had a new stereo that I could control, but I had no satellite hook up.

The next time I went back to Chicago I purchased a new antenna on eBay. When I got back I connected it with ease, but the music was going to be short lived again.

Rainstorms in Acapulco are like nothing I've ever experienced in Chicago. They occasionally cause the ocean to overflow onto the Costera. I was not aware how deep the water could get. One rainy day I was driving in front of the same spot where Fernando would later be killed, just west of the Hotel Emporio, when I encountered a tidal flow that would render my XM useless yet again. The water was over three feet deep. It reached the windows of my car. Driving through, it was inevitable that water would enter my car, and it did. The XM receiver installed under the passenger seat was ruined by inches of water that saturated my car.

On the home front, it didn't take long before I realized that, due to the enduring heat, electronic equipment was subject to strange forces in Acapulco. The clearest example of this was the Yamaha receiver I had brought from Chicago. I was living in my second apartment and dating Inés at the time. It was a warm evening, like they all were, and I was in my bedroom/living room listening to music. Suddenly there was a loud pop and the stereo fried out. It could have been anything, I guess, maybe a power surge, but I believe the cause was the heat, I did have a cheap surge protector connected at the time. When I moved to Acapulco permanently I brought as many high end surge protectors as I could.

Bicycle

While living in the tropics I wanted to have a bicycle. Every time I went to Sam's Club I saw their relatively large selection of bikes at typically low Sam's prices. I ended up buying a road bike there, a mid-priced model that seemed sturdy.

From the first moment I got it on the road it gave me problems. It didn't take long before I realized that, although it seemed to be assembled, it was not adjusted for use, there were many loose parts. Through Paco Muñoz, I found a guy who repaired and sold bikes out of his house. He lived 15 minutes away from me on bicycle. He adjusted it for use. I thought I would be set. I figured, if all the screws are tight and the chain and pedals are installed correctly, it would give me few problems. This was not to be the case.

In Acapulco I came to believe that all the poorest quality products were sold in Mexico, where regulations were lax to non-existent. This was strongly evident in my new wheels. Almost every imaginable problem arose with that contraption. The pedals fell off, were replaced, and fell off again. The chain fell off for no apparent reason. The tires went bad. When I rode it, my trips were often for the express purpose of taking it for repairs.

I eventually got tired of the guy Paco recommended, he seemed to be charging me too much, and often I would go to find him and he would be gone. I found another repair shop that was much more reasonable. I would pull up, the guy would repair my bike while I waited and charge me the equivalent of two or three dollars, five at most. Of the cost I could not complain.

Even though I had changed repair shops, the problems continued. I finally got so fed up with that bike that I abandoned it. I was right by Diana la Cazadora and it broke down again. Over a period of little more than a year, I had had the bicycle repaired at least a dozen times. I took the lock and water bottle holder I had installed, leaned the bicycle against the wall just downstairs from La Crissis, and walked away. Hopefully, whoever took it was an expert in bike repairs because that one was nothing but trouble.

A typical ride began at my apartment and went down the mountain. Heading west I reached Playa Manzanillo, near the famous La Quebrada, where the cliff divers have been doing their thing for decades. From there I would turn around and ride east to the Naval Base at the opposite extreme of the Costera. My route was a kind of a triangle with 60% of the Costera retraced when I finished. I would estimate the ride from home, to Manzanillo, to the Naval Base and back to my apartment was about four or five miles.

About 70% of the street corners had curbs designed for handicapped access so riding between blocks was not difficult. Nevertheless, there were plenty of places on my route where I had to take advantage of lower curbs or driveways to avoid having to dismount. There were a half dozen places where I was obligated to get off my bike because of a 8-10 inch high curb.

I rarely rode on the street, the sidewalk was much safer, but during tourist season the path would often be crowded. Generally, people tend to spread out side-by-side, blocking the entire width of the sidewalk when walking in a group. It was a challenge to navigate around them. They were oblivious to the fact that they were not the only people using the sidewalk. In Acapulco even motorized two-wheeled vehicles used the sidewalk, so I knew I wasn't breaking any laws on my bicycle.

I had a terrible experience once over near Playa Manzanillo where there is a tourist boat that boards a few times a day. I was going along very slowly because there were some people around, just fast enough to keep my bike from falling over. I came upon some young children walking on one side and adults on the other. There was space between them to ride through. As I proceeded along, one of the kids, about five years of age, abruptly turned and rushed over to an adult on the other side. He ran straight into my handlebars. I was terrified that he was seriously hurt or that his parents would try to sue me, or both. He was sobbing, but was uninjured. I apologized profusely and was assured no serious injury had resulted.

Last Drive North

The other time I drove up to Chicago was less eventful, but interesting nonetheless. I was on a mission for love, hoping to start a long term relationship with Dina, the girl I met while in the Windy City for the four Counting Crows shows in April 2008. I recruited Carlos Varela to accompany me to the border. He had family in Mexico City that he planned to visit on the return trip, which he would do by bus at my expense.

We were using a GPS I had, but still managed to get off course every so often. There were times when I would make a wrong turn and the device would tell me that the new route was going to shave significant time off the trip, sometimes as much as an hour. It was strange, you never know what to expect from a GPS.

We stopped for lunch, our only planned stop, at a funny restaurant in the middle of nowhere in Northern Mexico. It was an old school bus, remodeled to accommodate seats and a kitchen.

When we got to Nuevo Laredo I decided to take a different, new, international bridge, rather than the one I had used the other time I drove through. I had heard it was much less busy, so in theory it would save time. This was a big mistake. Although there were barely any people crossing there, so the customs and immigration procedures were much quicker, the seclusion of the place made it impossible for Carlos to catch a bus out of town from there. We had to retrace our steps and go to another more centrally located, heavily trafficked, international bridge. As we drove around we wasted a ton of time, three hours, or more.

In my frustration I was distracted and turned the wrong way as we left the border crossing. I made a u-turn and a cop stopped us. He was as harmless as a Mexican cop can be, took a typical, inexpensive bribe, gave me a short lecture on safe driving, and let us continue on our way.

When we reached the main international bridge, I drove around trying to find a place where Carlos could get a taxi to the bus terminal. I dropped him off when we found a taxi, there were not many around.

As I passed through customs, my car was stopped and an in depth examination was done, most likely because the car is so unique, and because it was loaded with my belongings. They didn't care that I had cats, but they did make me dispose of some fresh fruit I had brought.

Once I was on American soil again my plan was to drive to my friend John's house near Dallas. By midnight I was barely able to keep my eyes open. We had left Acapulco at about 3:00 a.m. I had been awake and driving for over 21 hours. I could not go on. Looking back, I marvel at the fact that I avoided falling asleep at the wheel, I had to pull my hair and slap myself in the face repeatedly to stay awake.

I found a rustic hotel, stopped, and checked in. I did not mention my cats at check-in. The hotel clearly stated their pet policy. There was a $100.00 fee for pets in the room. I didn't want to spend that money when I knew my cats and I would not damage the room, moreover, the hotel room was $75.00 so it was unpalatable to pay more than twice the normal rate.

After sleeping enough to recuperate for another long day's drive, I packed my cats up and, surreptitiously, put them in the car. I then went into the bathroom where I had kept them, got down on my hands and knees and cleaned up every stray piece of kitty litter I could see. It was a battle, but I left certain that I would not be discovered. Over the following weeks I watched for a $100.00 charge on my credit card, but it never came. I got away with it.

On May fifth, 2008 I arrived at Leo's building, I would reside in his front basement apartment, where I had previously lived from September of 2005 until January 2007, shortly after my mom died. I made it back to Chicago in record time, driving 36 of 46 hours and stopping only once to sleep and once to eat. Within a week's time my Celica would be rear-ended and severely damaged, by State Farm's calculations, the car was totaled. But it would live again. (It was always drivable, so it was wounded, but a two week stint in the body shop brought it back to life, albeit still visibly damaged, upon close examination.)

Carlos at the School Bus Diner

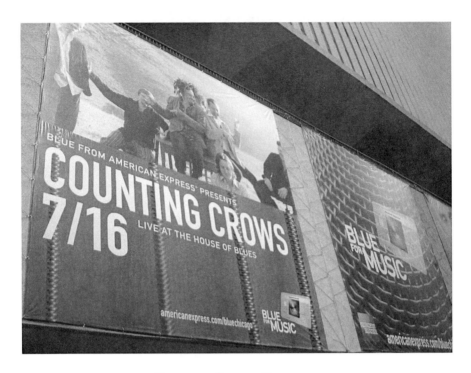

Counting Crows

Over the course of time between my initial move to Mexico and the day of The Phone Call, I saw Counting Crows 29 times. These were the 6th through the 34th times I have seen them.

I have been a fan since 1994 when their first album, "August and Everything After", debuted. My first Crows show was in July of 1994 and my second was a few years later in 1997. In 2002, before I moved to Mexico, I saw them three times, bringing the total up to five.

Less than three weeks before I first moved south, I was fortunate, and savvy enough, to finagle a pair of tickets to their private concert celebrating WXRT's 30th anniversary at Park West in Chicago. My co-worker's son was head of promotions for Budweiser's Latin American division and the show was sponsored by Budweiser. I implored her to help and she came through with a pair of tickets for me. As my Crows concerts continued to accumulate, my interest in the band grew in tandem.

The first time I saw them after moving was Adam Duritz' birthday, August 1st, 2003. I drove to Milwaukee with an ex-coworker from the University of Chicago, Stuart. He was a big Crows fan, too. We saw them at Marcus Amphitheater on the Summerfest grounds. It was a great show, but the next one was even better.

The July 4, 2004 show was outstanding for many reasons. I had come back to Chicago by plane for eight weeks to teach some classes at Truman College, earn some money, and see my family and friends. Chicago has an abundance of entertainment in the summer and the festival they played at is a prime example.

Counting Crows were playing for free at "A Taste of Chicago" on my favorite holiday of the year. I got there before noon and got in line. When they let us in I made it to the first row on the right side, in the seat closest to the center, one of the best seats in the house.

This was the 7th Crows show I'd been to in my life. I was still a novice when it came to the intricacies of the band, but loved them enough to make every effort to see them from the best seat possible, my typical modus operandi.

As one of the opening acts, They Might Be Giants, played, Adam came down and sat in the photographers' section that comprised a fenced in area in front of the main seats. I took pictures from my seat and saw a few people go up and talk to him. Adam's sister came and sat with him, and his nephew played guitar on "Hanginaround", their signature sing-along closing number.

This tour was my favorite for many years. It was in support of "Hard Candy", their 4th studio album, which I loved. It was at the top of my playlist on my bus rides around Mexico in 2002 when I went to Acapulco and Zihuatanejo on vacation. It took me years to realize how cool a song "Up All Night" is, and "Why Should You Come When I Call" also took time to grow on me, but now they're both favorites of mine. They played "Up All Night" on rare occasions, and never played "Why Should You Come When I Call" in 2004. Nevertheless, the songs that their sets were based around, "Rain King"w/"Raining in Baltimore", "Mrs. Potter's Lullaby", "Daylight Fading", and "Sullivan Street" were always superb. Adam's voice was in particularly good form, as were the song arrangements. I fell in love with "Four White Stallions" that day, I'd had the song since 1994 on a bootleg, but had never liked it too much.

During "Mrs. Potter's Lullaby" Adam brought the crowd into the song. When the line that began, "Hey, Mrs. Potter won't you..." he let the audience continue with "...talk to ME!". Being high, and a little drunk, I was enthusiastically screaming it out and raising my fist each time this part came up. There was a kid next to me who was about 16 years old. Whenever it came time to sing, I would provoke him to follow my lead. We were way into it and, being in the front, the band could easily see us.

I've always assumed Jim Boggios, their drummer, saw what I was doing because, at the end of the show, he came over to the edge of the stage and threw me a drum stick. There were more people at that concert than almost any other concert I've seen in my life, and he threw one drumstick to one person, me. On the way to my car I told people I ran into what had happened, it was an unforgettable moment. Some shows inspire you to go see the band again and again, that was definitely the case this time.

My second Crows show was not far off. It was 12 days later at the House of Blues. Again something happened here that made it extra special, while something else happened that almost made it a tragedy.

This show was sponsored by American Express, in fact it was a benefit for a program to keep music education in schools. Additionally, it was being filmed for broadcast on DirectTV. I was fortunate that it was taped.

I drank and smoked a lot and got into concert mode. I ignored the "no photography" rule and took some pictures. A big, scary, security guard came and told me to stop. Moments previously, I had seen my ex co-worker Stuart, and when the guy started to get in my face I passed the camera to him. That security guard was not playing games. He made me get the camera back and pulled me into the backstage area through a side door. He forced me to erase the pictures I had taken and threatened to throw me out if I took any more. I was shaken up, but not enough to obey. I took video and a few pictures from waist level, while in front row. He threw down the gauntlet, I had to resist.

When the concert was broadcast a few weeks later, I was in Acapulco with my Chicago-based DirectTV subscription and my Tivo and I watched myself dance to the melodies of "Mr. Jones" from 2,000 miles away. I always loved "Raining in Baltimore" because he sang about being "3,500 miles away, and what would you change? Nothing". I recall being back in Acapulco and going through the pictures on my camera and seeing the pictures I had taken, but barely remembering that I had seen the concert itself. Luckily they jogged my memory. The summer was so busy, it kind of a became a blur. Now I remember it well. It was one of four times I was at a Counting Crows videotaped concert. In two of them I am clearly visible and in one, at a barn in rural Iowa, I gave Adam a beer in the middle of their set.

First Row, Petrillo Band Shell, Chicago

My third time after moving was at my least favorite venue in the world. It is in Tinley Park, Illinois and is currently called, well, I don't even know. It was the New World Theater, then. This was one of the weakest Crows shows I've ever seen. Adam was very overweight, I had a shitty seat, they played a bunch of songs I don't like much, the venue is so bad, all that stuff combined to make me consider not going the next night. I had a ticket for Springfield, Illinois, about 3.5 hours south of Chicago. I said to myself, if this show was *this* lame, why should I drive so far for the next one? I was glad I did.

The following night they played "Goodnight Elisabeth", one of my most favorite songs. The set list was much more to my liking. They show was at the State Fair on the fairgrounds in the middle of a horse racetrack. The reserved seats were in the grandstands far away from where the stage was set up. I had a grandstand ticket, but it gave me access to the track, so I went down there to get closer to the stage. It was a rainy night and the track was quite muddy. There was a carnival set up on the grounds and when Adam sang "Mrs. Potter's Lullaby" it was more apropos than usual. (It has a lyric about ghosts of the tilt-a-whirl lingering inside of your head, and ferris wheel junkies spinning forever.) The drive to and from was uneventful, I parked for about $5.00 on someone's lawn two blocks from the fairgrounds. At the fair there was a large variety of ethnic foods, none of which looked very authentic at all. I had some Pad Thai. I regret that I could never find a copy of that concert because it was so good.

The next show, my fifth, was my first concert after my mother died. I had been living in Chicago for nearly two years by then. My financial concerns had subsided significantly and I was planning to move back to Mexico. I had something like 50 sick days accumulated with Chicago Public Schools and I would lose them all when I resigned. I wasn't going to let them all go to waste. I used one to go to Louisiana.

The performance was at the New Orleans Jazz Festival. It was my first time in New Orleans and my first Jazz Festival. My flight arrived at New Orleans mid-morning and departed the next day at 7 a.m. It was going to be a whirlwind trip.

From the airport I planned to go straight to the fairgrounds, I had no hotel booked. When I stepped outside, I saw a girl who I vaguely recognized from other Counting Crows shows and decided to ask her if she was going to the concert and, if so, if she'd like to share a cab with me to the venue. She said she was going to the show, but didn't want to share a cab because she was going to her hotel first. It turned out she was the band's website designer and she went by the name "Jules", actual name Alicia. It would be the first of many times we would speak. She is a genuine Counting Crows insider.

New Orleans food will forever draw me back, shrimp po'boys and beignets stand out most in my memory. I went to see a few bands perform, one outside and one indoors. In the early afternoon there was a torrential downpour. The fact that it was warm made the rain tolerable, but the outdoor music was temporarily suspended due to the storm. At about 2:00 p.m. the rain was very heavy. A bunch of us were standing under a tent set up as a misting station, like a very light shower. Because the rain was so heavy we were better off under the sprinkler than we were in open air.

By the time Counting Crows came on there was a puddle about two feet deep along a natural ditch near the stage. It tapered off about 50 feet back. The crowd stood on either side of it.

This was the band's first show in about eight months. Adam Duritz had lost dozens of pounds and looked as fit as he did in the "Mr. Jones" video. He was even wearing the same suede jacket he wears in the video.

The highlight of the show for me was a cover version of "Femme Fatale" by "The Velvet Underground" during "Goodnight Elisabeth". The weather ended up cooperating during the Crows' show, the most important part of the festival.

The final time I saw them before moving back to Acapulco I went to New York and saw them at Town Hall. They were filming their one and only DVD, to date. It took about three years for them to release it, but they finally did. The released portion is the first part of the concert when they did their first album, "August and Everything After", in entirety. So, the second CC video taping I attended was also incomplete in its officially released form, just like the DirectTV House of Blues show.

The next gig was a bit different. Adam Duritz was booked for a solo show in Baltimore, Maryland on February 1st, 2008, the only time he's done that. I wasn't going to let such a unique event escape me. As of May 2013, it still is the only time he's played a pre-announced solo concert.

In order to attend this one I would have to get from Acapulco to Baltimore. I was determined to make it to the gig on a shoestring budget. I spoke to my friend Sergio in New York with whom I'd seen Counting Crows three times before, once being the Town Hall show the year before. I knew he was tiring of seeing them, but he acquiesced and we got the tickets. I booked a flight out of Mexico City to New York, and a rental car for us to use from there to Baltimore. The day before the concert I took an early morning bus, a five hour ride, from Acapulco to Mexico City. The train from the terminal to the airport was out of service, so I had to take a cab the rest of the way. The other public transportation option the employees at the bus terminal suggested appeared untrustworthy. I made my flight and made it to New York, got my rental car and, using my trusty GPS, got to Sergio's apartment without incident.

In the morning Sergio and I drove to Baltimore, a three and a half hour trip. After checking-in to our hotel, we made it to the venue at about two o'clock. There was no line, but there was an early entry offer, which we purchased. We had a few hours to kill so we went to a bar/restaurant a few doors down. I drank more than I should have accidentally. I wanted to get high, but had no bud.

When showtime approached, we returned to the venue, got in line and were admitted shortly thereafter. We found a spot in front of the stage. It turned out to be one of the coolest shows I've seen him do, but because it was acoustic the audience talked throughout. I was fascinated to see him do rare songs and special versions, but a large portion of the crowd just talked the whole time. I recorded it, but my recording was pretty bad, as they often are.

After the concert, Adam was out on stage and there were very few people around. I blabbered out, "Why don't you ever come to Mexico?", and he replied that he didn't make those decisions.

When we woke up the day after the concert Sergio said he felt sick and wanted to rush back to New York City rather than check out Baltimore. After one more night at his place I retraced my steps to Acapulco. I spent about 24 hours getting from my home to the concert and back. It was worth it. This was the closest I may ever come to a "Devil and the Bunny Show", (rare, unannounced concerts in New Orleans, with Adam, one or two other Crows members, and other special guests, playing long sets and lots of covers).

Easter of 2008 I was in Chicago and rumors began to circulate about upcoming dates Counting Crows would play. First they announced an Apple Store mini-tour that would include a gig at the one on Michigan Avenue in Chicago on April 9th. This was a free show, open to the public. If I were to return for their concerts I was going to be there for sure. Then they announced a regular concert at Carthage College in southern Wisconsin, less than an hour north of Chicago. This was a lock, too. Next I heard they were doing a private gig, sponsored by Northwestern University, which would be held at the Riviera Theater where I had first seen them back in 1994. Oddly, it would be the first time I'd see them in a venue where I'd seen them before, if I could get in. Last, I heard about a taping of Soundstage at WTTW Studios in Chicago they would do on the 8th, the day before the Apple Store. The Riviera show was Thursday and the Carthage show was Saturday, four shows in five days, two private gigs and two public ones. It was an easy decision to return two weeks later.

As the schedule unfolded, I was torn by the knowledge that if I flew back for the two public shows, I might be shut out of the private ones. That would not be cool.

My sister Ann had worked for the same company for 17 years, since 1991, but she was now working much closer to home at Northwestern University, (NU). She had been there for only three months. Fortuitously, now I had an in at NU and could possibly finagle a ticket, if they were available to university employees, not only to students and faculty. Upon investigation we learned that they were available to anyone on staff, so she was able to buy me one. Three down, one to go.

Having lived near, and studied at, the place where Soundstage is taped, WTTW Studios, on Northeastern Illinois University's campus, and never having been to even one taping, I didn't expect to be attending that concert. I was a frequent visitor to www.countingcrows.com, so when I saw that they were giving away ten pairs of tickets I entered the contest. While I was back in Acapulco waiting for my return trip to Chicago, I got an email from Jules, the woman I had met in New Orleans, informing me that I was one of the winners. I was going to be at all four shows!

I was the fifth or sixth person in line at the Apple Store show and was shown on the Channel 5, WMAQ News that evening. Thanks to Tivo I have a copy of it. I was interviewed, but my travels from Acapulco to see Counting Crows four times were not what they wanted to hear about, so the interview never aired.

On Friday night I went to Lalo's on Clybourn Avenue and met Dina, who it turned out was born exactly 20 years after me, to the day. I fell in love with another girl who was arguably too young for me. She was to be the inspiration for my return by car in early May. When I look back on the time we spent together, I believe she was mostly interested in me so she could get a green card, but she did seem pretty serious and accepted my invitation to the Carthage College show the next day. I was ecstatic. In spite of being quite hung over, she went with me. She realized she was familiar with, and liked, the band when they played "Colorblind", a song she knew.

In Fall of 2008, Counting Crows were booked for the grand re-opening of the Wellmont Theater in Montclair, New Jersey. I was in Chicago visiting family and friends. The shows were scheduled for October 27th, 29th and 30th. My girlfriend, Sandra, who I had reunited with after the Dina fiasco, encouraged me to go, and my habit of traveling around the country to see them gained steam. The 29th of October was Sandra's birthday, but she understood my devotion to the band and, rather than deter me from going, was a catalyst in my decision.

I flew to LaGuardia from O'Hare in the morning and took an airport shuttle to Clifton, New Jersey where I stayed at a Howard Johnson Hotel. Soon after I checked in, I took a very expensive, short, cab ride to the venue. I got there about one o'clock in the afternoon and was one of five people in line. It was an ugly, chilly, rainy day. Around four o'clock someone came out and told us that Adam Duritz was sick and the show was being postponed until the next day. I was relieved that it wasn't scheduled after the others because this change had no effect on me, other than the need to commute one extra time between my hotel and the venue. Last minute issues with the Fire Department's inspection of the newly renovated building almost cancelled everything, but they were resolved by showtime the next night.

The concerts were some of the best I've seen them do. The band played 42 songs total, with only two songs repeated. I have soundboard recordings of all three nights, which gives me the opportunity to hear them in pristine form whenever I like. I met Ryan Ford and we started our Counting Crows friendship which has taken us to more than six states and about a dozen concerts since then.

I saw the band eight more times during my last two years in Acapulco, but in each case I was already in the U.S.A. on vacation, so the travel was minimized. On August 21st and 24th 2010 I saw them at Ravinia Festival in Highland Park, Illinois. I scored a first row, center, ticket for the second night and bought four more in fifth row, which I sold to cover the cost of mine. I was suffering from my second inguinal hernia at the time and would have surgery a day after the second concert. I was in pain and not able to enjoy those two nights as much as usual. It was not long before I would receive even more grave medical news.

Adiós Mamá

In October of 2005 my mother made one of a string of visits to her general practitioner, who, incidentally, was mine as well. The doctor did a chest x-ray. She heard nothing back from him so she believed that nothing abnormal was discovered in his examination. Fast forward 11 months to September of 2006 and she found herself in the emergency room with chest pains. As she and the doctor reviewed her test results, he asked her what she planned to do about the spot on her lung. That was the first she had ever heard of it. After living with it for at least a year, she learned she had advanced lung cancer. Less than five months later, on December 31st, 2006, she died. I was living in Chicago at the time and was able to be with her in the hospital during her final days.

My mother's internist claimed he had called her and left a message on her machine about the spot on her lung. This in itself was absurd. Couple that with the fact that she had seen him various times in the months subsequent to the x-ray, and it was clear he was grossly negligent. My sister and I found a lawyer and initiated a lawsuit in 2007.

Hernias, Cancer, and Bird Flu

When I had basic health concerns in Mexico, (sometimes not so basic), I would go to the clinic at a local pharmacy to get a doctor's opinion. This is how I learned I had one hernia, and later, another. I suffered longer than necessary because I did not want to have surgery down there.

For a number of weeks while teaching at the university, I had to explain to my students that I had a hernia that was unpredictable and painful. I would be in the middle of teaching and would have to apply pressure to my groin area as I could feel my intestine bulging out. I endured long enough to get the thing sewn up in Chicago.

I often bought temporary medical insurance policies in the United States to allow me access to medical care there. I was not always vigilant about keeping them active, but had purchased one for nine months at the end of 2009. I was due for a colonoscopy, a $5,000.00 procedure, and was not willing to pay the mega-inflated cash price that the American Medical Industrial Complex forces vulnerable Americans to pay. I took advantage of my coverage to have a hernia sewn up while on that policy. I went to my new physician for a check-up, too. I had other problems, like difficulty urinating, and wanted to get them checked out.

My new general practitioner, Dr. Sikorski, did something my old doctor, the one who neglected to inform my mother of her lung cancer, had never done. She sent me for a PSA test. It indicated my level was well out of normal range. I was sent to a urologist who did a biopsy of my prostate. Having a prostate biopsy is like getting stapled inside your colon, and this is done a dozen times or more. It is painful and the sound is frightening. Nevertheless, having it done saved my life, so it was worth it. The results showed that I had advanced prostate cancer. Coincidentally, I learned I had prostate cancer the same day that my sister and I learned that the lawsuit against my mother's doctor had been settled in our favor. It's hard to think of two more polar extremes. My temporary health insurance plan had ended on August 31st and I found out I had cancer on September 1st.

I went to get two more opinions about my prognosis and was told to either get chemo and radiation treatments or have my prostate removed. The last doctor I spoke to said he was conservative when it came to surgery, but that in my case it was the only good choice. I believed him.

I tried to get the insurer to renew my policy or continue my coverage. Ultimately, they refused to cover anything. My insurance agent told me that I could probably have obligated them to pay if I had had the surgery immediately, but having one's prostate removed is a major event that can leave a man debilitated in critical ways. I was not ready to risk losing my ability to have sex without having sex at least a few times more before then.

I got multiple opinions on what the best way to deal with my illness was. I determined that a prostatectomy was the correct option to ensure success. I had my prostate removed November 3rd, 2010, when I was 45 years old. My doctor used a DaVinci robotic device to assist with the surgery. He had done thousands of these surgeries before. I knew there was a significant chance I would be impotent afterwards. Weeks after the surgery my sister told me that, as I gained consciousness after anesthesia, I asked her repeatedly, "Did he save the nerves?". I have no recollection of that, but am sure it's true. I can't imagine what life would be like now if I could not have sex, there are enough negative side effects to the surgery, that would have been hell.

When the initial H1N1 (Bird Flu) virus scare occurred I was back in Mexico, it was early 2009. I have overreacted to some threats and this is one example of that, but I have an aversion to dying of some avoidable stupidity. This was an entirely new virus and, according to news reports, people were dying; young, healthy people. Until the powers that be had some kind of handle on the matter, I wanted to reduce my exposure to the danger. The entire country was gripped by fear. People were advised to avoid physical contact with those around them. The cultural norm of a kiss on the cheek was shunned for fear of spreading the disease. Handshakes became fist bumps, hugs were exchanged at a minimum.

Many of my friends in Mexico see the whole thing as a conspiracy between the Mexican government and the medical profession. They say their intention was to control people through fear while also selling medical supplies, like surgical masks. I believe that the threat was real, albeit much less dangerous than what we were told by the press.

Over the initial period of time when public knowledge of the disease was nebulous, I got pretty paranoid and spent some days at home, avoiding contact with all human beings. One day I made a rapid excursion down to the Bodega Aurrera to buy some food items, but spent days on end at home before and after. In retrospect, I acted pretty nutty, but when a new deadly disease is discovered in your back yard, it can be disturbing. Ultimately, it was revealed that the illness was far less fatal than originally declared, so life slowly returned to normal.

Moving House

When I made my most permanent move to Acapulco in August of 2007, some stupid shit went down. First I had to get a visa. I had had one that allowed me to work at the university, but when I moved back to Chicago in August of 2005, I just let it expire.

In addition to the visa I'd have to complete a *Menaje de Casa*, an itemization of what was being moved and its provenance. Brand new items were virtually forbidden, and other things were prohibited too, but I didn't learn exactly what until I received my shipment, minus those items. When filling out the *Menaje de Casa* I had to specify where I got what, and when, with special detail provided about the more expensive items.

The Mexican Consulate in Chicago provides visas and *Menajes de Casa*. I went there with all the documentation I understood was necessary and got an unpleasant surprise. According to the man I spoke to, I had to renew my visa at the place where I had gotten it before. I had to make a pre-trip to Acapulco again, similar to my initial six-month trial in 2002-2003. I got a ticket and flew down and went directly to the consulate. When I finally was attended to I was informed, to my chagrin, that, since my visa was expired, I was starting from scratch again. I had no reason to be there, I had merely wasted my time and money based on the ignorance of the consulate employee in Chicago.

I flew back to Chicago and went to the consulate again. In the interim, the man I had spoken to had been dismissed. His replacement had little sympathy for the time and money I had squandered. I was back to square one. I reapplied for a visa and it was granted a few weeks later.

I finally got my paperwork in order and found a moving company that I thought I could trust. It was hard to find a company that made international moves, but I did. On the day of the move I had some things ready and other stuff, not so much. I wanted to avoid the extra fees for having them pack things, so I tried to box my new 42" flat screen TV myself. I did a pretty pathetic job of it and I marvel at how it arrived relatively unscathed. In the months after the move, it had a weird issue with shows that had green screens, the colors would form blotches on the screen. Eventually the problem remedied itself and the TV still works wonderfully to this day, seven years after I bought it.

While the company was packing up everything I was shipping, they inadvertently moved things that I was not. There were things in the house that were staying there that didn't technically belong to me. One of these was a large chair with a wood and wicker frame, and gold colored velour pillows. It had been in my parents' living room for decades. A few minutes before the movers arrived, I dropped my Ray Ban sunglasses and they slid under the gold chair. When my glasses fell on the floor, I said to myself, "that chair is not being moved, I know exactly where they are and won't misplace them if I leave them there". In the confusion/pace of the move, the movers packed the gold chair. I immediately noticed it was gone and informed them that it was not being shipped. They brought it back, but one of them snatched my sunglasses. There we were, three of them and one of me and it was an indisputable fact that one of them took the glasses. In spite of my pleadings and certainty that one of them was a thief, none would ever admit it, lying to my face, looking me in the eye. I never saw those glasses again. My complaints to the company were fruitless.

Pizzas and Baked Goods

Besides the dozen or so pizzas I carted down with me over the years, I also shared some of my mom's baking. I took breads and cookies she baked, eating some myself, while sharing others.

In my first few months in Acapulco, I entreated my parents to send some cookies through the mail. Their disdain for my decision to emigrate was exhibited in the way they sent the package. The cookies were in a plastic bag, but they were placed in a box with no other packing in it, so they slid and bounced and rolled around through numerous postal workers' hands, trucks, and shipping stations. By the time I got them they were largely reduced to crumbs. I ate peanut butter cookie crumbs, not pretty, but still delicious.

After my mom passed away, I took over and made some of the things she had made so well. The banana bread I made, through vicarious maternal tutoring, was always a big hit. I still have people ask me for loaves. I was also renowned for the French Onion Dip I made. In the United States it is quite common to find this dip at parties and holiday gatherings. It is about as simple as can be, requiring nothing more than a pint of sour cream and a package of dry soup mix. The thing is, for some strange reason, that soup mix is not sold in Mexico. I made a big impression on many people with "my" French Onion Dip and was often asked for the recipe. It boggles my mind that no one has had the business savvy to sell that stuff down there, it is very popular and would certainly sell in abundance. Every time I go I take a few boxes to work my magic with my special dip.

Dining

In Acapulco I ate out far more often than I ever did in the United States. A full meal can be had for less than $5.00 and there was an abundance of options at every turn. Most dining locales had limited menus, offering one, two, or three choices, so it was important to decide what you wanted to eat before you picked a restaurant.

At Manzanillo Beach harbor there were half a dozen seafood restaurants. My girlfriend Inés took me to one of them a few months after we started dating. After trying two or three of them I found my favorite. It was called Mariscos Zerimar. They had three main flavors of salsa, all of which I loved. There was an oily red one especially for seafood, a thick green one, and a red one made with *chile de árbol*.

When I first started eating there I would go twice a week, or more. Their salsas and seafood selections, accompanied by flour tortillas, made every meal scrumptious. I couldn't get enough. Over time my budget required me to curtail my visits, but I continued to return often. I was such a frequent client that some memorable moments occurred there.

One day I was out partying near the university and I met a few women I liked. I invited them to go there for dinner with me. Since I didn't know them well I was embarrassed to ask the cab driver how much he was going to charge us to get there. This was one of the very first things my ex-wife Angélica had taught me when I went to Mexico on vacation years before. You should never get into a cab without agreeing on the price. The ride was ten minutes long and should have cost 40 pesos on the high end. When we got there the driver said it was going to be an outrageous sum, something like 120 pesos. I was angry and wasn't willing to pay. Richard, the owner of Zerimar, came and helped me argue with the guy. He got the driver to reduce the cost by one third, but I still paid more than double what the cost should have been, it sucked.

I always raved to the owner about how much I loved their salsas. Over time I became a *cliente* and got to know his wife, Nancy, the chef. She offered to teach me how to make a few of them. We made a list of ingredients that I would need and, a day or two later, I came back with them. I had to go to the main street market, el *mercado* aka "Tepito", to get some rather obscure chiles. We spent a morning making salsas and I wrote down the recipes.

My contact with Richard, Nancy, and the restaurant ended abruptly in early 2010. I went for my usual meal and ate a dish that I had eaten many times before, with a liberal portion of salsa to top it off. At the time it struck me that the green salsa, which was normally fresh and warm from being out on a table or waiting to be served, was cold, indicating it had been refrigerated. It tasted fine. It was not. Without going into specifics, I had the worst upset stomach of my life. By the time the sun rose the next morning I had entirely cleared my system of all solids and liquids and my weight was down by seven pounds.

It took me until 2015 to return. Everything was still delicious. They had changed the name of the restaurant. Richard and Nancy were happy to see me again.

Besides Zerimar there were a few other restaurants I frequented. A couple served *comida corrida*, (fast food, technically), but were, more precisely, kind of fixed price for a complete meal. Many of them charged a mere 20 pesos for a drink, usually *horchata*, limeade or *agua de Jamaica*, soup, a main course, and tortillas, often homemade. I alternated between one place or another. There were groups of them situated around stalls in the souvenir and arts & crafts kiosks. Since I always had a full hour for lunch at the university it was no problem to go and eat a relaxed meal.

One of the places I went was known for its roasted chicken. It was popular among students and teachers alike, so it was not uncommon for me to run into co-workers or students there. I loved their salsa and always consumed it in excess. Over time their salsas had a weird effect on me that deterred me from going back, let's just say they caused me indigestion. It always struck me as funny how that restaurant invariably served lukewarm, or cold, tortillas. They bought them in the morning and put them into an ice chest which was frequently opened as orders went out. By lunch time they weren't very warm at all.

The eatery that I considered my favorite, where they made some of the best, freshest tacos and quesadillas I have ever eaten, technically had no name, but was commonly known as Las Cazuelas (The Casseroles). Two things made their food exceptionally delicious to me. First of all, unlike the roasted chicken place, their tortillas were the freshest I have ever eaten. They made all of them by hand and they got multiple deliveries of *masa*, (dough), throughout the day. They also had delicious salsas, one red and one green.

Arriving at Las Cazuelas, you saw six wooden stools facing a short wooden counter top. On the counter were clay pots, or casseroles, (6-10 of them), lined up, some with clay lids, some with plastic plates used as makeshift lids. Frequent customers like me would walk in and lift the lids to see what taco/quesadilla fillings were available at that moment. I never had a bad meal there. Over time I got to know the woman who owned it, and her daughter and daughter's young sons. I gave them banana bread I baked and once gave them a hand mixer when theirs broke. I inspired the owner to start selling quesadillas with *chiles rellenos* as the filling because I requested them often. They were very popular and, more than a few times, she was kind enough to save me one or two when she knew I was coming and expected to sell out. I told her about how my ex-wife had made me *chiles rellenos* with a different kind of chile, *pasilla*. Two or three times she made those chiles especially for me, but did not sell them to the public.

While she did treat me kindly most of the time, I had some difficulties there, too. The restaurant was located about a half a block from a government office where I paid my Federal taxes annually. When their employees had their lunch hour they would overrun the small diner and fill it to capacity. This seemed to happen on days when I took a friend with me to eat there. We would sit down and wait and wait and wait and, whether our order was taken or not, not get served. It was annoying. I got up and left once when I went with Carlos. Objectively speaking, I understand why they had to focus on their principal clients, but I was one too, so to be ignored was exasperating and my friends couldn't appreciate the place when we never got any food.

On Thursdays in Acapulco the law says you must eat *Pozole*, a pork and hominy stew which originated in the state of Guerrero. Well, maybe it's not the law, but it is quite popular, and I went to pozole shows regularly. I would often go to a place called Los Anafres, (The Grills), with my friend Miguel Acevedo and his friend Miguel Garcia. Everyone called Garcia *El Tocayo*, (namesake). The restaurant was owned by a friend of Miguel's so we always got preferential treatment. We would bring a bottle of scotch or rum and they would keep us steadily supplied with fresh glasses and ice. The waiters would even pour our drinks. The shows were fun. They had a comedian who I liked, usually I could understand most of what he said. There were dancers who had extensive, colorful wardrobes and a couple who danced *Pimpinela*, a misogynistic dance in which the couple argues and feigns physical violence. It was amusing, albeit outdated and very politically incorrect.

The food was served from an open buffet with two or three types of pozole, condiments like fried stuffed chiles, pork rinds, *chalupas*, (bowl shaped chips with pork filling), *queso fresco*, crispy, flat tortillas, and gelatins. At diners' tables was a plate of different dried chili powders, sliced radishes, sliced avocado, and oregano.

Another restaurant I enjoyed on occasion was a place called Ika Taco. I had a friend who worked there named Mauro. He was rap and reggae master Yó M.C. Youalli G.'s cousin. Ika Taco was known for fish tacos. They also had an extensive selection of salsas; coconut, papaya, and peanut, to name a few. When you sat down they brought out eight or ten salsas and explained what each one was made from. I loved the variety they offered but the chips they used were far from best. They were round chips purchased in bulk. They did not make their own chips or even use ones that seemed to be homemade. It was a defect that I never understood. I asked Mauro and he said the owners felt that making chips was too laborious and time consuming. It was a classic case of missing that one final, crucial step to achieve greatness.

Some of my other favorite places to eat were street taco carts that were basically permanent businesses. One of them was parked about three blocks west of Paco's taco cart, on the street where I scored bud with Fernando one time. This locale was so popular that the line would often reach more than a dozen people. They had about ten varieties of tacos *de guisado*, (stewed), or otherwise prepared fillings. If you didn't arrive early your choices would be limited. Filling options were *barbacoa*, (barbecued beef), rice with hard boiled eggs, blood sausage, mole, *huevos con chorizo*, *salpicon*, and more. Condiments were available from giant vats of salsa, plates of avocados, and bins of radishes with pickled peppers and onions. Patrons would stand around the cart and eat, or sit at the long picnic tables set up nearby.

This spot was so popular that they eventually created a new arrangement. In one line you would pay and be given a little ticket that stated how many tacos you had purchased. You then walked around to the other side of the cart, waited in another line, gave your ticket to the *taquero,* and told him what fillings you wanted for each different taco.

There was another, similar, cart run by a lady over near the Convention Center. It was very popular too, but was never as crowded, being located in a spot with far less foot traffic and adjacent businesses. Since it was much farther from where I lived I went there far less frequently.

A well known seafood restaurant I went to every so often was Los Buzos, (The Scuba Divers). They had three or four locations around Acapulco. The ambiance was interesting. They had 15 foot high ceilings with murals and artifacts related to the sea, and diving, adorning the walls. I usually ate *Pulpo Enamorado* or *Coctel de Camarón*, (Octopus in Love or Shrimp Cocktail) there.

The many Sundays I spent at Chalio and Nefta's restaurant, El Palmar, were a mix of tequila or rum, and fresh seafood, often *huachinango*, (red snapper). An entire red snapper cost about $12 and was a delicious feast for 2-3 people. *Huachinango a la talla* is red snapper prepared with a red sauce. Miguel Acevedo, the manager of La Crissis and I would meet there in the early afternoon, I'd bring a bottle of rum or Corralejo Tequila and we'd order some of their wonderful fish. Eventually, Chalio and Nefta had a disagreement with the owners of the space and moved to a spot adjacent to that one. Their new restaurant, El Morro, was much larger and more appealing. For a while they had live music a few nights each week at the new spot.

Kitty corner to Paco's taco cart was another cart that only opened during the daytime, Tacos Chemis. They sold *tacos de canasta*, (tacos from a basket). These are something I didn't try until I lived in Mexico. They are quite small and an order is usually five tacos, but it is easy to eat as many as ten or more. The heat they maintain after preparation is what keeps them warm all day. The tortillas are very soft and can be crumbly from the steamy cloth and basket they are kept in until sold. Chemis had picnic tables with awnings for customers to dine at. They were always busy and sold until their day's supply was gone.

Down the street was another daytime cart where they sold *tacos de barbacoa*. They gave you a cup of scalding broth and a tiny spoon with each order, plus radish, avocado, and all the salsa you wanted. They were open on Sundays when other carts were not, so I frequented them that day more than others.

Another half block down there was a fresh juice stand that prepared your juice as you waited. A large cup of orange juice cost about a dollar and they often gave you a banana to go with it. They had pineapple and a bunch of other fruits that you could mix and match for your special concoction.

Dining in Acapulco was never fancy, but it was delicious in its simplicity. Eating outside almost every day of the year is a treat.

Mariscos Zerimar

Nefta, Marcelo, and Isra at El Morro

Bus Crash

Public buses in Acapulco are a sight to see. The common colors are blue and yellow. Many yellow buses say "Maxitúnel" because they take riders to the other side of the mountain through the maxi-tunnel, charging an extra fee for the convenience. These vehicles have turn-styles in front so you must exit through the back. On most buses when passengers wish to disembark they shout out, *bajan*, ("they get off" literally translated), and the driver stops soon after to let you out.

More than half of the buses are not air-conditioned, and the ones that are charge a higher rate. Certain drivers own the bus they drive, so they deck it out accordingly. This can be comical as well as annoying. It is not uncommon to see buses that have music so loud it causes their windows to shake. Many buses are painted to the whims of the owners. Some have voluptuous women in skimpy outfits or lingerie adorning the vehicle. Others are designed for the owners' children, painted with cartoon characters or superheroes. A fair percentage of them are very poorly maintained. They expel black clouds of exhaust and make breathing difficult for all in their path.

On the lateral road to *Avenida Cuahuahtemoc*, a main thoroughfare, a taco cart was always stationed. It was situated just across the street from the Corona Beer plant which also doubled as a bus stop. As soon as you passed the Corona factory and the taco cart, the road rose steeply, so buses would have to accelerate strongly to get up the hill. Those were the "exhaust tacos" to me because they were terminally bathed in the smoke and fumes that dozens of buses pumped out as they passed by. I never ate there.

I was pretty lucky to not be involved in any serious car accidents during my six+ years residing in Mexico. But I was hit by a city bus once on *Cuahuahtemoc* fairly close to the *mercado central*. I was chugging along in afternoon traffic and bam. Out of the blue a bus changed lanes into me. My beautiful Celica's left, rear quarter panel was partially shredded by the spikes coming out of the bus's wheel.

Another way the bus drivers tricked out their vehicles was to put any of a variety of spiky posts on the lug nuts of their wheels. I don't know if the intent was to look cool or menacing, but when one of those things comes in contact with a car, it slices it up like a tin can. The damage to my car could easily have been worse, but it was still bad. I managed to get the guy to stop before he gouged my tire and car any more.

When you have a car accident in Acapulco you stop and wait until a *perito*, technician, arrives to assess the situation. He does all his official bullshit, like drawing chalk lines on the ground that serve no purpose whatsoever. You also stop traffic for as long as it takes to get the matter cleared up. When you are on a main thoroughfare, it seems to last forever.

For some inexplicable reason both drivers are always at fault in car accidents in Mexico, however in my case, more blame was assigned to the bus driver, in spite of him claiming I turned toward his vehicle and hit him. Once an accident occurs the involved parties immediately work out a fair compensation and exchange funds, as necessary. After we finished with the *perito* the bus driver and I went to a body shop and got an estimate for the repairs. He then gave me the money to cover them.

The damage to my car would have been over $1,000.00 if it were to be repaired right, but that was not what would be done in this instance. The guy gave me about $150.00 and we went our separate ways. A few days later I took my car back to the body shop and left it for the work to be done. When I had the car repaired correctly in Chicago a few years later, the work they had done in Mexico actually made doing the proper repair more difficult.

Slippin' and Slidin'

When it rained in Acapulco the downpours were often torrential. My Celica was not made for driving in the mountains. Nor was it made to handle the intensely slippery surface that was created when there was a layer of water on the asphalt or cement.

On two distinct occasions I had near accidents that arose as a result of skating across the road with my car. Once I was on the final approach to "El Campanario II", about a quarter block down from the restaurant. Carlos was in the car with me. There was a natural river flowing across the pavement and rain was pouring down. All of a sudden the car was not going up, but rather going down. It was terrifying. I didn't want to slide down the mountain, I didn't want to crash my precious car into object, man, or beast. By combining Carlos' coaching with my knowledge of how to drive on snow covered ground, I was able to calm down and proceed slowly enough to get over the hump and past the slippery section of the road.

The other time I was driving the disorganized and poorly paved maze of avenues on the west side of my apartment. There was heavy traffic on Cuahuahtemoc Avenue, the main thoroughfare, so I chose to try a back route that I was unfamiliar with. I rarely drove in that area because the streets tended to dead end or double back on each other, so it was possible to spill out where you started, rather than where you intended to go. Some of these streets were nearly vertical climbs, too, a very bad undertaking in a blinding rainstorm.

I was with Inés and was losing my temper rapidly. We were physically very close to my apartment, but logistically, quite far. The road rose at close to a 60 degree angle, and had narrow, sharp angled turns. I was nearly at a point where I couldn't figure out how to get through to my condo, although it was within sight. We began the ascent only to slide backwards to the bottom of the hill. I was freaking out. I didn't know where to go or how to go there. I calmed down and retreated to where I had begun without damaging my baby or getting stuck. So much for shortcuts.

Gas consumption was a constant concern to me because my mileage was exponentially worse there than it had ever been in America. I considered every explanation; the heat caused my car to burn gas more quickly; some of it evaporated while sitting in my tank; the gas itself was adulterated so it could never yield normal mileage; climbing mountains burned gas at a greatly accelerated rate. Eventually I decided it was probably all of these things, with uphill climbs as the likely number one suspect. I got about 30% the mileage there that I got in Chicago, it was remarkable.

Roaming Vendors

In Acapulco there are a variety of folks walking the neighborhoods selling their wares. Because my street was a dead end, and secluded, more than half the vendors in the neighborhood never approached my building.

There were *paleteros* who wheeled their freezers filled with *paletas*, (frozen popsicles), and there were others who peddled fresh, hot tortillas.

On certain days of the week the gas truck would make its rounds with one of the crew crying out "gas" at the top of his lungs while the driver honked the horn incessantly. Most homes had small tanks that had to be replenished every few weeks. My 300 liter tank lasted me six months at a time, so I didn't buy from them. I had to call the office and have them send the *pipa*, (tanker).

When the truck arrived they had to back it down my street because it is so narrow. Upon reaching my building they would send a guy up to my roof with a long rope. He would drop the rope down to his co-worker who would attach the truck's hose so the guy up top could pull it up and connect it to the tank. Mexicans have told me that those guys always adulterate the readings on their meter so you don't actually get the amount of gas they charge you for. I always checked the meters and the receipt, so the theft was never evident, if it did occur.

Gas station attendants were no more trustworthy. In Mexico gas stations are all full serve. When buying gas the attendant will always say "ceros" before beginning to pump, to indicate the meter is at zero. People say some gas stations are more honest than others. I almost always went to the same one, it had a good reputation for some reason. It was also close to my place, straight up the mountain to *Calle Ruiz Cortines*.

One of my favorite street vendors is the *bolillero/a*, (bolillo man/woman). A bolillo is a small roll. The bakery where they made bolillos was at the end of my block, but it did not sell retail. Each morning and evening a cadre of men, women, and teenagers, would arrive there, pick up a large basket of bolillos and head out to his/her territory nearby. Ironically, because my street was more or less a dead end street, I lived there for years before any of them traversed it, as they called out, *bolillo*. There was one woman who had a very twisted way of saying the word, almost incoherently, and Inés used to make fun of her. She was the woman who was most often designated to sell to my immediate vicinity, but never once went down my street.

The day finally arrived when some new, younger vendors came onboard. They did pass down my street, often at the end of their shift/basket. It was not unusual for them to give me a few extras, if not double what I paid for. They were going back to the base and wanted to get rid of all their product. This was their last chance to do so. On occasion I would see a pile of bolillos dumped half way up my block. I got the impression that the bolilleros were instructed not to return with any product.

In the evening, a woman and her teenaged daughter sold tamales from a small boxlike container on wheels. She never came down my street either.

Once a month, or so, a man would come around blowing a small whistle. He was a knife sharpener. Each industry had its trademark sound.

The first year I was in Acapulco there was a small shop at the bottom of Calle Bora Bora where they made simple sandwiches and fresh squeezed juices. Around the corner from there was Auria, who had a kitchen in a giant metal box. These locales were common in town. Coca-Cola, or some other vendor, would set up a metal structure that housed a kitchen. Auria, was from Oaxaca. She was an attractive woman about my age. Most of her clients were men. She made two or three dishes per day. You paid 25 or 35 pesos for soup, drink and a main course, *comida corrida*. Whatever you ordered came with a half dozen tortillas. It was a great value, although it was the same idea as the other *comida corrida* places where I ate, Auria's food was of higher quality, it was more like home cooking.

A block down from there a woman set up a small table in front of her house and sold fresh juice in the morning. I bought from her a number of times. Her stand did not last too long, though.

In the same vicinity, there was a grocery store, Comercial Mexicana. I had a friend there, Marcella, who worked at the package check booth. They do not let you carry packages into stores in Mexico. I would spend extended periods of time there talking with her. She was married so we never went out. I kept in touch with her after I moved back, and we still exchange messages from time to time.

In front of Marcella's little cubbyhole there was a woman who sold *elotes* and *esquites,* (corn on the cob and corn off the cob with mayonnaise, lime and chile powder). I enjoyed many a cup full of *esquites,* but after about 2010 almost none of the ladies who sold them were around anymore.

There were also trucks that cruised the neighborhood every so often, about once or twice a month. One of them called for discarded large household items, like mattresses or appliances. Some collected metal and would pay cash for what they took. I sold them some metal tubes and other miscellaneous pieces I had from the construction I did on my condominium.

When I first moved in, I was in urgent need of an *herrero*, what we call in English, a "smith"; a person who works with metal. It is standard procedure in Mexico to cover all your windows with metal bars. The new construction my condo was in did not have anything other than glass in metal frames. Plus my front door was a hollow wooden utilitarian model, which provided almost zero security. My acquaintance from Frontera Grill, Fernando, had a cousin whose wife resided in Acapulco. This woman was one of few people I felt were *de confianza,* (trustworthy, honest), there, and I had had great difficulty in finding an *herrero*. She hooked me up.

I had him install bars on the small windows in my apartment, four in all, as well as in the three holes that the builder had created in each bedroom for window air-conditioning units. He forged a front door for me, too.

After the main bars were installed, I realized that I needed wire mesh put on the windows, otherwise animals could enter from the neighbors' roof, and my cats could get out through the bars on the front door. Carlos Varela put me in touch with another *herrero* who put a heavy gauge wire mesh across the lower part of the front door, and on all the windows' bars.

I chose to leave the three large windows, one in each of the two front bedrooms and the one in the kitchen/living room, un-barred. Since my unit was on the third floor, it was unlikely that a thief would climb up to gain access through any of those windows, the smaller ones afforded much easier access from the neighbors' roof. Later, when I installed a window air-conditioning unit in my bedroom, I removed the grill he had installed there and recycled it with the metal-collector.

Security was not the only reason I needed to get bars and screens on my windows. The roof of the neighbor to my east was the same level as mine. Any animal that got up onto their roof could easily enter my apartment. I vividly recall, one night, waking up to go to the bathroom and seeing a cat almost fly out of the bathroom, across the living room, over the kitchen window ledge and down 15 feet to the cement border wall at the side of our parking area. I could not let strange cats have free access to my space.

Over the years quite a few people came to work on my apartment. Through Pépe's wife I also found a gentleman named Plutarco. He was a carpenter. He built my bookshelves and two closets for me. He also built the cat carrier box I intended to take on airplanes, but never used, and the boxes for my albums, which I relegated to carrying almost anything except albums. I did send one of them, filled with LPs, with the movers. It was surprisingly heavy when loaded with its intended cargo.

Those boxes were a challenge to move no matter what they held, the wood would cut into your hands and the rope handles were equally as bad. I wrapped rags around the ropes to make them more tolerable. At Home Depot in Chicago I found some plastic discs that adhered to the bottom of the boxes, meant to help move furniture, and took some back with me when I moved back permanently. I slapped them on the bottom of those boxes and voila!, they slid across the floor with ease. Those sliders made a world of difference when I needed to move the crates. They even saved my hide when my friend Ted gave me a bulky behemoth of a television while I waited for my belongings to arrive from Mexico. That television weighed a ton and had no handles of any kind. I placed the TV on top of the box and slid it from my car, to the elevator, and into my apartment.

Another task I gave Plutarco was to make some screens to use in my three large picture windows. I was terrified that my cats would get up on the bedroom or kitchen window frames and fall over to the other side. It was a 20-30 foot drop to inaccessible rooftops below. The idea was to avoid having my breathtaking view obstructed by a screen, so I had screens made that I could easily see over. They covered the lower third of the windows.

When I moved back in 2007, Squeaky, now full-grown, was back at his birthplace. As I unpacked, he found his way up onto the kitchen window ledge before I knew it. I hadn't replaced the screen there yet. I approached quickly, but cautiously, so I wouldn't scare him into jumping. He had managed to walk onto the ledge area that was behind permanent, stationary glass. As I reached for him he went down.

I raced downstairs and found him in the same spot where he had landed after a 20+ foot fall. I feared he'd bolt, I feared he'd have broken a bone as Hamlet had done falling from the terrace 15 feet above. I grabbed him up in my arms and was delighted to find he was completely unharmed, shaken, but intact, an immense relief.

My Building

End of My Street, Patricia's Car

Sex and Pornography

It did not take long before I began to feel the subtle undertone of sex, (maybe not so subtle), in Sunny Acapulco. Tabares was the first thing you would hear out of a taxi driver's mouth when you asked for an entertainment recommendation. I went through my strip club phase back in the late '90s in Cancun, I had seen it all, so I was not looking for that kind of fun.

On my first two visits I inevitably took taxis, always asking the driver the cost before I got in. I got charged an "American tourist" surcharge, but generally I wasn't gouged too much, I knew I had to pay more, I just didn't want to pay double the proper rate. Once I adjusted to the lay of the land, I knew what the price range should be.

I often asked the driver where I could meet women and he always responded with "table dance". When I explained that I didn't mean that kind of women, sometimes they would point me in the right direction. Copacabana was a salsa dance club where I ended up on both of my short vacations in August of 2002, I liked it and returned every so often until I heard it was run by scary folks. True or not, I wasn't interested in finding out the wrong way.

Acapulco had a thriving sex industry that had a reputation for having no restrictions, the city was perceived as a sexual deviants' haven. During the first year I lived there a large international child pornography ring was busted, they were awful people doing awful things and their capture gave the impression that, thankfully, there were at least some limits to what one could and couldn't do in this beach paradise.

He doesn't deserve all the blame in the matter, but Carlos Varela was very instrumental in getting me to patronize strip clubs more frequently than I wanted to. On rare occasions I went with other friends, but Carlos instigated things more than anyone else. His wife Chantal's brother worked at Foxy's, and the manager, Jaime, also Carlos' friend, would give us free or discounted drinks. Frankly, I strongly disliked going there. I always told Carlos, if we are going out, I want to be in a place where there is at least a modicum of a chance that I will meet a woman I could fall in love with. At a strip club, that was not going to happen. Many nights we divided our time between those joints and regular bars. Foxy's was noteworthy for the ongoing arrangement they had. Any man who was willing and able to get onstage and have sex in front of the public was welcome. I saw few takers and fewer who were successful in their intended act.

I won't say that I didn't like the entertainment, and it was nice when I saw a woman I liked and she would come, drape herself over me, and let me buy her an outrageously overpriced drink. A lesser man's ego would be stroked, and his anatomy might be too. I never had sex with any woman I met at Tabares or Foxy's or any other strip club in Acapulco. Over the entire eight years I resided in Acapulco I went into those traps between 20-30 times. They remain at the bottom of my list of entertainment options.

In spite of my nominal interest in table dance, I did go to Tabares once with Chango. We had nothing particular to do and we found ourselves nearby, so we went in. It was a mistake. The management always perceives through osmosis exactly how much money you are carrying. Your check always tends to drain you of your funds, but somehow not exceed the amount you have with you. However much you go in with, you end up spending it all, with a few pesos to spare. It's amazing.

That night Chango and I both met girls we liked, I liked mine way too much. Things got relatively hot and heavy there in our booth. Ignoring the locale of her employment and seeing it from a purely physical standpoint, this girl was just what I wanted. I got her number and called her a few times, but we never saw each other again.

Recycling

It was a challenge to recycle in Acapulco, but I gave it a shot. I saved all my containers; aluminum, plastic, and glass; bottles, cans, and boxes. I learned that there was a place in Costa Azul that accepted paper, plastic, and aluminum for recycling. Every so often I would drive over there with my trunk full of containers, milk boxes, etc. When I turned in my stuff, I got credits for food stamps, depending on the weight of what I brought in. Items were divided and weighed and you were given a receipt that told how much credit you had. When I learned that I could donate my proceeds, I did. On my fourth trip to drop stuff off I was told that they were no longer accepting anything there, the program was being re-organized, and would be off line indefinitely.

The recycling office did not accept glass bottles, but I did save mine in hopes that I could get a glass collector out to to my apartment to take them off my hands. The people I found would only pick up very large quantities of bottles, so I was unable to recycle mine.

I once bought about eight cases of Grolsch beer, in the big, flip top bottles. I couldn't believe they had it at Sam's Club, so when I saw it, I bought as much as I could. I gained 20 pounds from drinking all that beer, and it took me years to get my weight back down.

Whenever I had something to throw away that I thought someone would like, broken electronic equipment, clothing, etc., I would place it prominently at the end of my block. It would inevitably be removed before the garbage collectors came around.

Trash collection brought another truck to the neighborhood. Each truck had a guy who would walk around the area, on the blocks the truck was imminently arriving at ringing a cowbell. That was the signal for garbage collection, a steadily ringing cowbell. Because my block was long it was nearly impossible to distinguish from what direction voices shouting, bells ringing, or horns honking came from, we would leave our bags of trash at the mouth of the street and the garbagemen kindly picked them up.

When I lived with Señora Silvia, it was never easy to get my trash onto the truck at the right time. It was forbidden to leave piles of trash around, although they would spring up on trash day. The year I lived at the top of Bora Bora Street I found myself chasing the garbagemen often.

One of the coolest things I saw in Mexico was in Mexico City. Hector took me to meet his cousin who was a creative person with handyman skills. He had built a waterless toilet in his house. It used a series of natural filters and had a structure similar to an outhouse. The toilet itself was nothing unusual, but inside it had a large open space which housed the filters. Although waterless toilets have existed for decades, if not centuries, it is not common to find one. I only wish they were the norm rather than the exception. In Acapulco alone the water savings would be immense.

Condominium Sale

When 2016 started I never imagined it would be a year in which I would ride a wave of unpredictability and uncertainty month after month. I would spend 10% of the sale price of my condominium traveling to Mexico a total of seven times in an effort to close the deal.

In late 2015 I had been back in Chicago for nearly five years. The year ended on a sour note, not only did I not get my hip replacement done as planned, but I did all the pre-surgery prep and none of it was covered by my insurance. I never expected that the bad luck would carry over into the new year, but it did, in spades.

I began 2016 by doing most of the hip replacement prep again, some parts were still valid in the new year, donating blood for myself was not one of them, however, so, I donated blood for myself, twice, and saw my dentist and doctor and was cleared for surgery.

Dr. Beigler operated on my right hip on January 13th. Everything went as well as could be expected and the pain was minimal, I didn't even need any medications once I got home, other than an occasional Tylenol. I had in-home physical therapy for a while and a nurse came almost every day to check the viscosity of my blood. It was too thick for a few days but once it was at an acceptable level, no more nurse visits, no more blood draws, I was on my way to health.

A few days before surgery, on January 10th, I got an email from Alejandro, my real estate agent in Acapulco. He had found buyers for my condo. They were offering $680,000 Mexican Pesos, (MXN), which at the time was $33,331.00 USD, but I was supposed to kick $80,000 back to the buyer for repairs and expenses. I rejected the offer. They countered by saying that I wouldn't need to pay the kickback, so we had a deal. I naively thought the sale would proceed rapidly and smoothly.

My first trip down to Acapulco to sign paperwork was February 29th through March 7th. I was told that the paperwork would take seven days to complete, so I made sure I'd be in town long enough to do everything required of me. After having been off work the majority of the year so far as I recovered from surgery, I took more time off and went down to sign the papers.

The drug war and its corresponding violence became worse than ever in Southern Mexico in 2015. Acapulco was the worst area, having reached a murder rate so high it was ranked as the fourth most violent city on Earth, (not including places actively engaged in war). The violence encompassed every aspect of daily life in Acapulco, touching the lives of nearly everyone in the port city.

On the day I arrived I went to an afternoon meeting at the notary office. It turned out to be the same place where I had finalized the purchase of my condo back in 2004. The details of the purchase/sale were explained to me and I was advised that the paperwork would be completed the following Monday, so another meeting was arranged for that day. I left thinking all was in order and everything I had to contribute would be done before I left town seven days later.

Since 2011 when I left, as the danger in Acapulco intensified, my desire to go there diminished correspondingly. I made every effort to stay as briefly as possible and I tended to stay in my hotel room at night. In 2016 there was a new phenomenon in which the combatants were shooting up taxi stands. One day I went to Mariscos Zerimar at Manzanillo Beach. It is located at the opposite end of the bay, about two or three miles from my hotel, the Emporio. Between the time I went to the restaurant and returned, the taxi stand in front of Soriana Supermarket, located on the Costera between my hotel and the restaurant, was shot up and four people were injured including a young girl. No one died immediately, but one person expired a few days later.

On this trip I managed to see my friends Miguel and Miguel. We went to Los Anafres for the Thursday night pozole buffet and show. An inebriated performer, acquaintance of the Miguels, sat down with us and shared our bottle of whiskey. She tried to latch on to our party and wanted to join us at our next destination, but she was broke and already a little tipsy, so we told her we were going home. We left and went to Las Trancas, a blue collar bar with live music and dancing that Miguel and *El Tocayo* often frequent. We drank, watched the continuous stream of bands come in, set up, play, and depart, danced a bit, and watched NBA basketball on the TVs hung around the dining area.

The next night I managed to build up the nerve to go see my friend Beto who was playing trumpet for a band at a place called Combat Wings, near Baby-O. It was great catching up with Beto and the band even mentioned me by name during their set. I gave Beto a glass straw and took his picture for my website, strawwarsusa.com. He invited me to his upcoming wedding in January of 2017.

For the remainder of my stay I laid low in my hotel, walking to Chemis to get tacos *de canasta* each morning, while stopping for a fresh squeezed juice at the stand adjacent to the tacos.

On Monday we had a second meeting at the notary's office. The lawyer in charge said she did not think that my bank account, based in the U.S., would be acceptable for the bank that was giving the buyers a loan, but she did not say "no" definitively. The buyers were using an *Infonavit* which is a type of government loan extended to citizens based on their work history. I figured, a bank is a bank. Alejandro and his associates were under the same misconception. I was scheduled to leave that afternoon, so I did.

Within two weeks' time the other shoe dropped. Alejandro messaged me with the news that the buyers' bank was not going to deposit into my foreign account. This was to be a very serious and expensive obstacle to overcome.

Over the last five years many international banks have been in the news, among them, possibly the worst, was HSBC. The reason for the headlines? Money laundering on a global scale. How does this affect me? It has caused the banks to tighten their rules and make them stricter than they've ever been. I have no doubt the drug traffickers still launder their billions in the same manner as before, but when it comes to the little guy, things are much more involved than they used to be. Much, much more.

Back in 2003, within a month of moving to Mexico, I got a bank account at the HSBC that was practically on the Universidad Americana campus. It was as convenient as could be, but banking there was ultimately a poor decision. It was a very simple process to open the account. In 2010 I decided there was no point in keeping that account open, so I closed it. It had been sitting there with a few pesos in it, inactive. This turned out to be a serious mistake.

In 2004 I paid about $1,000.00 USD to open a trust for my condo purchase, no foreign citizen is allowed to own property within 10 kilometers of the ocean in Mexico. I went to the bank I knew best, where I was already banking, HSBC. No one at the bank knew anything about setting up a *fideicomiso* (trust account). I never considered trying any other bank, though, I figured they were all the same. After a fair amount of finagling with headquarters in Mexico City, the bank officer, and her assistant, Sarita, got the thing done. I had to pay an initial fee and my annual payments were to be $500 USD. This was August of 2004. When I moved back to the U.S. in 2011, I, somewhat mysteriously, got contacted by a company called Nezter that was a receiving agent for HSBC in the U.S. I was to make my payments to them while outside Mexico.

Even though it never seemed to be urgent, I always paid my trust payment on time, or within a few months after the year ended. I had difficulty about five years into the deal when my account number changed. It was a challenge to get the new information, and I had to do so in Acapulco, but a bank officer eventually got it for me by making calls to Mexico City.

In 2012 I committed an apparently innocuous error. To this day I have no idea how I let this happen. I put the old account number on the yearly payment check. It would be years before anyone could rectify the error. My contact with Nezter was Adriana. She spoke English fairly well, which I prefer when talking on the telephone. When the error was discovered she got in touch with her contacts at HSBC. It was determined that my payment had been applied to another account. This did not seem like a major issue for the bank to resolve, but it took a bunch of phone calls and emails between all parties involved before my account was credited correctly.

Over time I learned that Scotiabank is the best, possibly only, bank in Acapulco, that sets up *fideicomisos* locally. My life, and the sale of my condominium, would've been *much* easier had I chosen to use that bank.

Upon learning that my American bank account was not going to work for receiving the buyer's funds, I was up against an obstacle that would cost me thousands of dollars and several weeks' time. It did nothing to help my standing at my job, either. My first step to resolve the issue was to find out if there was any way to open the account without going back to Mexico. This was quickly proven impossible. Next I had to determine with absolute certainty what the requirements for an account were so I would not make another futile trip to Acapulco to open it. After asking a few friends down there to go to banks and verify what potential account holders were required to provide, I learned that I was going to need a visa for Mexico. Since the overwhelming majority of Americans do not need a visa to go there, those of us who do are few and far between. I figured that owning property there would be sufficient reason to be given one. I couldn't have been more wrong.

The first time I went to the Mexican Consulate in Chicago I arrived early in the afternoon only to discover that the visa department closed at 1:00 p.m. every day. The consulate is located on South Ashland Street, so it is a 90 minute roundtrip, minimum, every time I go there. The distance and schedule made it difficult for me to go there without rearranging my work and exercise schedule.

The second time I went there I arrived well before 1:00. I went through the security check point and over to the office where visas are handled. There was no number system for those who needed to see the two, (usually only one was present), women in that office. The "system" was, you would duck your head into the office and tell them why you were there, they would tell you to take a seat in the five rows of eight chairs outside. Either Karla or Lillian, the visa women, had to remember who came in what order, and you had to struggle to make sure you didn't let anyone who arrived after you get ahead. Wait times were usually 15-30 minutes.

Karla was the woman in the office this day. I, oh so naively, told her my story. It seemed only logical that they would understand my situation and give me the visa, as an owner of property in Mexico, it never occurred to me that they would deny me one. She told me that she had encountered other people who were in the same predicament that I was, but it was a complicated matter that someone in the Mexican Government would have to resolve, because they did not give visas to people who needed them for real estate and banking transactions. I immediately took a different tack. I told her that I would apply for a six-month visa and I asked her what the requirements were for that. She explained that I would need copies of my bank statements for the last six months that showed I had the economic solvency required to prove I would not end up being an indigent in Mexico. Karla looked at my passport and saw that the pages were nearly all covered with stamps and previous visas, so she informed me that I would have to get a new passport that would have blank pages on which they could place the new visa. I knew I could provide the bank documents, and getting a passport takes time, so I left, disheartened, but certain I could overcome their obstacles. This was the last time I saw Karla.

The passport took about three weeks to obtain, I paid for expedited delivery. It cost over $200 in total. The bank statements took a lot of ink and paper, but I printed most of them at home. Approximately a month after seeing Karla, I went back again.

On this visit I met Lillian, she didn't seem exceedingly bright. I presented her my visa application, the deed to my property, six months of bank statements, and my brand new passport. I also brought the pictures needed for the visa, taken at Walgreens on the way to the consulate.

For some reason, (my big mouth?), I opened up to Lillian and told her about my property sale, too. She saw my huge stack of bank documents and other things and shuffled through them to see if my bank balance was high enough. Then she took everything and left the room. When she came back she said this wasn't enough, I would need a letter from my boss stating that I had permission to take a six-month leave. I was frustrated, but had no other choice. I knew my boss was cool and that she would provide the letter for me. I got it as the next day and went back to the consulate as soon as my schedule permitted.

Lillian was the only person in the visa office once again. I showed her everything and she said, no, this was not going to work. I had told her that I needed the visa to open a bank account and this documentation was not proof of anything different. I became irate. I told her I would request a permanent retirement visa instead. She told me I'd need a letter from my boss that said that I was quitting. This was about the stupidest thing I'd ever heard. I told her, it's a free country, I can quit whenever I want. Nevertheless, she told me to get the letter and I said I would.

My boss, Dena, came through again. She gave me this absurd letter and I told my co-workers that if anyone happened to call and ask if I worked there anymore, they should say I did not.

Coincidentally, on April 8th, between the first and second times I met with Lillian, my dear cousin Mary died suddenly and entirely unexpectedly. She was 56 years old. She was like a second sister to me. It was a heartbreaking shock to everyone. Since I am a bad liar, I decided to use this tragedy to my advantage. When I went back to the consulate I saw Lillian again. I was still in shock over Mary's passing. I told Lillian that my situation had changed drastically, my cousin, who was like a sister to me, had suddenly passed away. I was devastated and was going to move to Mexico again. I showed her all my documents. She took them and left again to confer with someone. As she left I asked her if she had ever had a death in the family that affected her profoundly. She seemed mildly sympathetic. This time when she came back she said that she couldn't give me a visa because I had told her at first that I wanted it to open a bank account. I would have to re-apply in six months. I implored her to understand that my life had changed. She didn't care. She is exactly the type of person who proves to me that the most dangerous people on Earth are those with small brains and lots of power.

I left dejected but not defeated. There had to be another way.

My first idea was to go to another Mexican Consulate in an adjacent state, either Wisconsin or Indiana. As I investigated I discovered that the one in Wisconsin had yet to be opened and, according to reliable sources, the Indianapolis one was actually a satellite of the Chicago office which would mean they send visa requests to the office where I had been rejected. Michigan's office was farther away and in a city I was unfamiliar with. No other consulate nearby seemed feasible. I decided my best option would be San Diego. I had wanted to visit there for years, it had a functioning consulate, and it was 20 minutes away from Tijuana, so I thought I could just bolt down there once I had the visa in hand. Little did I know that things had changed in the way visas functioned since I last got one.

I got online intent on putting this nightmare behind me while subverting the morons at the office in Chicago. The website for San Diego's Mexican Consulate was encouraging, it was the exact opposite of Chicago's. They not only had a clear order of procedures, but applicants were required to make a reservation online. I immediately made one for May 2nd, about ten days after the current date. I would fly to San Diego the 1st of May and go to my appointment the next morning.

Before I left I reverified all my bank statements and other documents, all I had to reprint was the visa application. I was a little concerned about the fact that all my documents had Chicago addresses, but I figured they would have no reason to suspect I wasn't a local if I was applying there, in San Diego. I booked a room with AirBnB and used that address as my address in California on the application itself.

Arriving early for my appointment, I signed in and took a seat. I felt like I was committing a crime after my experience in Chicago, it was hard to smile or relax. The woman who I spoke to was somewhat surprised that I was moving to Mexico. I avoided letting my ulterior motives cross my mind, but I am a very reluctant liar and was constantly worrying that I would be found out. I knew that I was doing nothing harmful to anyone, but I still disliked having to be less than forthright.

As she reviewed my documents it became evident that I had stumbled a little bit. I had applied for a retirement visa because of my experience in Chicago. I didn't have confidence that they'd grant me a short-term visa, so I went for broke. It turned out that the retirement visa is actually only for people who are on Social Security. Luckily this was easily remedied and she helped me change my request accordingly. I told her I planned to leave for Mexico as soon as I got the visa. She took my documents and pictures and told me to return two days later at 9:30 a.m. to pick up my visa. Success!

Once I left there I decided to go to Tijuana to try my luck at opening an account without the visa. I had nothing to lose. I drove straight south and found parking near the pedestrian entry point to Mexico. From there I followed the signs to enter the country by foot. It wasn't difficult to see which way to go. There were two or three folks walking along ahead of me. It was a very brief walk, less than five minutes, until I reached a huge portal above which "MEXICO" was written. It amused me no end to see a door that says Mexico on it. My second excursion of 2016 into my old home country was underway.

Entering Mexico

Passing through customs and immigration, I had so few belongings with me that they let me go in without pressing the button that activates the stop/go light for customs. Outside there were a few taxis nearby whose drivers charged higher rates for more comfortable vehicles and more luxury service. I kept walking toward the cheaper ones down the street. I told my driver to take me to any Bancomer branch. He took me to the *Plaza Financiera*, the financial plaza, where there were three or four banks. The Bancomer was under construction, and closed. I walked down the street and saw an HSBC behind an expanse of parking lot so I decided to try there.

Mexican banks are very busy and slow paced, (well maybe not so busy, but definitely slow paced). On the client log book, I wrote down my name and the issue that brought me there and took a seat. There were two or three people ahead of me. When my turn came I was assisted by a young man. I told him I wanted to open an account. He said I needed a visa and the ID card that comes with it. I was not familiar with the card because that aspect of the visa did not exist when I had obtained my visas previously. I told him I was a customer with a *fideicomiso* at HSBC. He didn't care. I told him I was a property owner in Mexico, he didn't care. I showed him my property title and passport, but he told me he could only open the account with my visa and the ID card that went with it, plus two documents showing proof of residency such as a phone or electric bill. He said I'd need a letter of reference, too. I had an awful copy of my water bill which he indicated would not be sufficient. I left disappointed, while maintaining hope that I could get the account at another bank. There were two others in the block.

Next up was Banco Santander. They had an open area with tellers on one side and bank officers on the other. Between the two there was a woman who appeared to be management because her desk was situated between the two principal areas. I signed in and sat down. After a 15 minute wait my turn came up and the woman in the center area called me to her desk. I explained that I wanted to open an account. She said that she could open it with an official copy of my electric bill, another document showing residency, and a passport. I thought I was dreaming. I had a receipt from CAPAMA, the water company in Acapulco, a copy of my electric bill, and my passport. However when she saw my electric bill, she told me it was not sufficient because it was not an official copy. I was excited because this looked like the best possibility for opening an account. Since the electric company is national I could go there immediately. Once I got a copy of my electric bill I'd open the account and wouldn't even need the visa. I just had to go to the electric company and get an original copy of my bill. This would be easy.

I went out on the street to get a taxi to La Comisión de Electricidad. Luck was with me, the main branch was a five minute drive away. I got in line and waited to see the person who directed clients to each different department. When my turn came they gave me a number and told me to take a seat in the waiting area. After ten minutes I was called to the window. I told the guy I needed an official copy of my bill and he found my account. The irresponsible Alejandro, my real estate agent, had not been paying the bill so I had to pay an outstanding balance and a reinstatement fee. I had almost no cash with me so I had to track down an ATM. I found one a few blocks away.

When I had gone to Acapulco in February 2016 my American bank account had been frozen due to possible suspicious activity, in fact it was me who was trying to make a withdrawal. They didn't even let me do one transaction before they froze it. It was a big pain to get remedied and I spent $20 on an international call to the U.S. I had advised them of my travel plans this time and, miraculously, they didn't block my account so I got some cash.

I returned to La Comisión and went straight to the guy I had seen before. He tried to pull up my account and was unable to. There was some sort of disturbance in the system and he could not connect to the office in Acapulco. I was cursed. He had me take a seat while he tried to remedy the situation. After 15 worrisome minutes the system came online again and he printed my receipt. But it was in black and white and did not look entirely official. More obstacles. They had no color printer there, but he was able to email me the file so I could go print it in color myself. Before leaving the office, I went to another window and got a date and time stamp on my receipt so it would be as official as possible.

Now I had to find somewhere to print the damn receipt in color. I wandered along a main roadway in the vicinity with few businesses in sight. After a few blocks I stumbled upon a small strip mall. There was a little convenience store/

pharmacy that gave me hope. I told the guy what I needed and he said he could print for me. Between customers and fiddling with his computer and printer we got it done. It was a full sized piece of white paper with the receipt printed in the middle and three inch borders on all sides. On my way out the door I asked him how to get to the financial center, he told me it was on the other side of the expressway immediately beyond a mall's parking area. There was a bridge with a sidewalk where I could cross. I walked back to Santander as quickly as I could, took a seat, and waited for the woman I had spoken to to become available. First she was attending to a woman who seemed to be trying to cash a check. The process took forever, with the bank officer making more than one phone call to deal with the matter. When she was done a man walked up and spoke to her before I could, I was angry. This caused another ten minute delay. As he finished he asked me if I had been next and apologized when I said yes.

I showed the woman my documents, fully believing that I had found the Holy Grail. When she looked at them closely she saw that my residence was in Acapulco. She informed me that their policy was to send someone out from their branch to verify residency. In other words, only local people could open accounts there. She suggested I find someone to let me use their address so I could be considered a local. All I needed now, it appeared, was an electric bill of someone who lived in Tijuana or nearby. I rushed off to La Comisión again to try my luck at finding someone who would let me use their bill. This was going to get strange.

I retraced my steps to the office and watched as people arrived to pay their bills. I asked friendly looking people if I could give them 500 pesos for a copy of their bill. Those who answered me said they were paying someone else's bill so they couldn't give it to me. I retreated in shame, feeling like a fool, when no one would accommodate me. This was obviously not meant to be, another dead end.

Since I was in Tijuana already, I figured I'd try one last bank, the Banamex next door to Santander. Their lobby was packed, but they had an efficient number system, so I took one and sat down. Before I was attended to, a bank official asked me what I needed, I told him why I was there and he said the same things the others had, I needed a visa, so I thanked him and left. Obviously I was going to need to get the visa before I could open an account.

I had 40 hours before my next consulate appointment, but I had every reason to believe the visa was forthcoming so I could enjoy my time in San Diego. I watched the Cubs game on TV at Rosie O'Grady's, a Chicago themed sports bar, and enjoyed a little home away from home.

When Wednesday morning came around I was in the same nervous mood. I arrived a little early for my appointment and signed in again. This was unnecessary, after a few minutes a different woman called my name from the other side of the waiting area. She seemed surprised at my desire to relocate as the other woman had been, but sent me to the next window to pay, $36.00. No $100 bills accepted anywhere at the consulate, apparently they believe only drug dealers use the $100 denomination. After paying I went back and gave her my receipt and passport. She took them and told me to take a seat. She had to walk the passport to another office and get the visa stamp in it. Within ten minutes she was back. Before giving me my passport she told me in no uncertain terms, the visa was valid for one entry, and one entry only, into Mexico. Upon entry I had take it to Immigration to get it *canjeada,* (exchanged). This was a new step for me, I had never done that with any previous visa. She gave me my passport. It had a stamp similar to the others I had gotten for previous visas. But this time it was technically incomplete and not activated.

Since I had the same visa stamp in my passport as each of the previous ones I had gotten, I convinced myself that it would be enough to get someone to open an account for me, either they would bend the rules or they would be ignorant of the new card that accompanied the stamped passport. As I had done 48 hours earlier, from the consulate I drove straight to Tijuana. I could almost feel the account within my grasp. After repeating the steps I had completed on Monday, parking, walking into Mexico, taking a taxi, and getting to the financial center, I went straight to Banamex.

I took a number, sat down, and waited. About a half hour after I got there, the same man I had spoken to the day before informed me that a banker would be available to speak to me shortly. A few minutes after that I was invited over to a woman's desk in a glassed-in cubicle. I was nervous but excited, I was about to get the account I needed. I told the girl that I wanted to open an account and provided her with all the documentation I had been told to bring. She looked things over and told me I did not have what I needed. I would need the ID card that goes with my visa, two original proofs of address, and two letters from acquaintances who could vouch for my character. It seemed she was pulling shit out of her ass to make it impossible for me to open an account with her. Nothing I could say or show her was sufficient to get the account open. My plan was thwarted again.

I left immediately and went to the liquor store to buy some tequila to take back home. I would go back to Chicago briefly and then fly down to Acapulco and get this done there, or so I thought. I was not going to stay in Tijuana for an indefinite period of time while my visa was *canjeada,* being completely unfamiliar with the city made it an easy choice not to stay.

I must mention, in my defense, two days previously when I had gone to Tijuana, immigration did not stamp my passport, this made me think no one would be any the wiser that I had entered and exited.

I arrived in Chicago at 8:18 p.m. Saturday May 7th. My friend Bruce picked me up and drove me home, saving me a few hours which the bus would have taken. Once home, I unpacked, washed clothes, repacked, and left early the next morning.

My flight left at 3:10 p.m. but security delays were the biggest news story of the day, so I had to get to the airport at least three hours before my flight. This was probably the least anticipated trip to Acapulco of my life, therefore I scheduled it so I would be arriving at 11:19 p.m. on Sunday the 8th of May and leaving less than 48 hours later, at 7:39 p.m. on Tuesday the 10th. All I planned to do was activate my visa, go to a bank, open an account, provide the account information to the lawyer at the notary's office, and get the hell out of there.

First thing Monday morning I went to the immigration office in Acapulco. I was one of two people there and was attended to quickly. The girl was friendly at first. She took my passport and began to process my visa. She gave me the impression that she was somewhat surprised that I was moving to Mexico permanently, as had the women in San Diego. After examining my passport closely, her attitude changed. She told me that the stamp on my visa indicated that I had entered Mexico with it before arriving in Acapulco and that this would make things more difficult. She said immigration would have to get authorization from the location at which I had entered before my visa could be exchanged. I played dumb and said, ok, whatever it takes, I understand. I also told her I'd need permission to leave because I had a sick uncle, (since my uncle was 91 years old, I used poetic license to proffer a logical reason why I had to leave immediately). She printed paperwork for me to fill out in order to be allowed to leave before the visa exchange was completed. She also printed the documents I needed to legally validate my visa. Lastly she told me to go to Walmart to get pictures for my visa. Everything seemed to indicate the "mistake" of re-entry I had made could be remedied. I left to get the pictures. When I got back she told me to return the following day for my exit/re-entry permission.

A dark cloud permeated the office when I returned the following morning. I had expected to be given permission to leave with the understanding that my visa would be processed and available for me upon my return in a few weeks' time. The congenial girl of yesterday was gone, today she would barely look at me. She said, "you entered and left without exchanging your visa, we have to cancel it". I was shocked and heartbroken. I was barely able to focus as I sat there for what seemed an eternity while she drew up the papers to nullify the fine work I had done in San Diego. The voice of the woman who gave me the visa repeated over and over in my mind, "this is valid for one entry, and one entry only, into Mexico". I thought I could get away with breaking the rules. After well over a half hour, she had me write out a statement confirming that I had broken the rules and was renouncing my visa. It was a sad day. After what seemed to be an eternity, the paperwork was done and I was free to go. I left with my tail firmly planted between my legs.

When it came to acquiring a visa, I was an expert now, so I quickly got online and booked another appointment at the Mexican Consulate in San Diego. There was nothing available until May 31st. I scheduled it for 8:00 a.m. knowing this might be difficult and would certainly be my final chance to do this right.

That afternoon, I arrived well ahead of time for my flight from Acapulco to Mexico City, but after waiting a few hours, I learned it was cancelled. The airline said it was a mechanical issue, but judging from the fact that I was one of only three people who got sent to a hotel, I think it was more a question of using an empty jet to fly us, or putting us up for a night. Once again I ended up at the Grand Hotel, just like when I tried to escape the people who threatened my life in January of 2011. I had paid for an upgrade on the Mexico City to Chicago flight, so now I'd have to hassle with the airline to get my money back or get it applied to another trip.

Once back in Chicago, I again printed out the visa application and the most recent calendar month of bank statements as proof of my solvency. I was tempted to book my room with the same guys I stayed with in San Diego before, but their place was a little on the expensive side, and it was a ten minute drive from the bars I knew I'd be hanging out at. I have been told that in California you spend something like $15,000.00 for a DUI, so I did not want to risk any such thing, especially since I now knew the lay of the land. I found a room which seemed like a good deal within a mile of Rosie O'Grady's and El Zarape. It turned out to be a very small room with no TV and doors which were actually curtains. I could hear the host's snoring at night, so it was not an ideal place to stay. I was able to walk to wherever I went on excursions at night, though.

I arrived promptly for my 8:00 a.m. visa appointment on May 31st. This time I was received by a man at the window where I turned in my documents. He was kind of a jerk. He said I needed my bank statement for May. I told him I did not have it because the month wasn't even over yet. He took my paperwork and advised me I'd need the May statement on Wednesday, which would be June, when I had to come back to pick up the visa. Just what I needed, another obstacle that could be insurmountable. This gave me something to fret over for the next 48 hours. My bank issues statements five business days after the month ends, so I could not provide an official one two days later.

When Wednesday arrived I went to the consulate early so I could stop two doors down to print out my balance as of that day, it wasn't a statement, but it was as close as possible. I walked around Little Italy killing time until my appointment, documents in hand. This was it, do or die.

I entered the consulate, emptied my pockets and turned off my cell phone, as required by security. I went upstairs to the visa department, wrote my name down as a precaution, and took a seat. This time there were quite a few more people there, nearly all Mexicans, with a few Americans thrown in. When the woman called me to the window where the visa is completed, I felt embarrassed and made a joke about how I had done exactly what she told me not to do. I had a story in mind to explain my stupidity, but it was not necessary to give her any reason for my error. She took my passport and sent me to the next window to pay. After doing so, I returned to hand her my payment receipt and took a seat.

The clock stood still as I waited for her to give me my second visa. All kinds of crazy thoughts went through my head. After 15 minutes or so, she came back and called me up to the window. She was very nice and understanding. She gave me her name and email and told me to contact her if anything went wrong. I had my visa and this time I wouldn't screw things up.

Unaware of more logical options, I chose to take a ridiculous route down to Acapulco. I could have gone to Tijuana and taken a direct flight, but I was unfamiliar with this approach and didn't want to mess around in Tijuana again. I attempted to take a bus up to Los Angeles, but was unsuccessful in finding one that fit my schedule. I called Thrifty Car Rental and asked how much it would be to drop my car off up there. The agent said I could take the car back to the San Diego airport and get another one as a one-way rental. The girl at at the agency was helpful and let me keep the same car. There was a charge for dropping off in another city, but she waived it, so I ended up spending about $75 to drive up to LAX. The distance is 125 miles and it can be driven in two hours, but traffic cost me two more, so I made it in just under four hours. My flight was at 11:01 p.m. and I got to the airport at 6:00.

After a lengthy wait for Aeromexico to open their check-in counter, I was attended to by a nice guy who told me he was from Acapulco. It turned out his uncle owned the bar I frequented most when I first moved down there, Mangos, in the Condesa neighborhood on the strip, an interesting coincidence. He said he used to hang out there when he was a kid and we determined that we may have seen each other there back then. I asked Aeromexico for the upgrade that I had been unable to use previously and they applied it to this flight, thus making a lengthy journey more tolerable. The agent was very accommodating and he gave me a pass for the Air Canada VIP lounge that Aeromexico shared with them. This was a real stroke of luck. The lounge was fully loaded with an extensive bar, a beautiful food and salad bar, wifi, televisions, and comfortable seats. It was superb.

When flight time came I was feeling good, although I knew I would have a long layover in Mexico City, I also knew I'd be comfortable in Aeromexico's VIP lounge where I had been a number of times on previous trips. The flight arrived at 4:45 a.m. and my connecting flight was at 11:45 a.m. seven hours later. I proceeded to the lounge and was informed that my upgrade, purchased by bidding, was not valid for entry into the lounge. I couldn't believe it. I tried to argue my way in without success. I had been very fortunate to be given access to the one in Los Angeles.

Discouraged, I proceeded to the boarding gate area and found a place to stretch out on the benches. I got very little sleep by boarding time.

Before I left home I had arranged a ride from the airport with my friend Miguel. It was urgent that I get to the immigration office the day I arrived so I could give them my documents as quickly as possible. I was booked to stay a week in order to assure that I'd get the visa exchanged during my stay and still have time to open the bank account. I had been traveling for almost 24 hours by the time I reached Acapulco. My flight arrived a few minutes early. I had told Miguel to be there at noon because my flight arrived at 11:45 and I didn't want him to have to wait. Regrettably, wait is the only thing he would do. As I exited the customs area I looked for him among the people waiting for arriving passengers, I did not see him. I went straight outside so I could find him at the curb and be on my way. I looked and looked for him in the parking area as well as the drop-off/pick-up lane. I waited until 12:20, knowing that the immigration office closed at 1:00 and my time was elapsing quickly. Finally I concluded he was not coming, in my exhausted state it never occurred to me that we had missed each other inside. I paid for a taxi and told him to take me to the immigration office. As we drove I told him what I was up to. He said he'd wait for me while I went in to the office, that way I wouldn't look so suspicious, running in there unkempt with my suitcase in tow. I figured I'd give him an extra 100 pesos, the charge to get to the immigration office from the airport was quite high already.

When he parked outside the office I hurried in, presented my documentation and was given a receipt to take to a bank to pay the visa fee, $1,600.00 pesos. The girl told me to go pay and come back. They would be closed but were still available to receive documentation on matters already in process after closing. I ran a few blocks east to the closest bank, went in, waited for ten minutes in line, paid, and was given a receipt for the payment. I ran back to immigration and gave it to them, along with the pictures I had taken the last time I dealt with their office. I was informed that I'd be notified by email in a few days with a specific day for me to return to pick up my visa.

The taxi driver did wait for me, and he did take me to my hotel, but he wanted another 300 pesos for his time. There was no way I was paying him a total of 1,000 pesos. We argued in the driveway of the Emporio. I gave him 100 pesos more than the original fare from the airport and walked into the hotel with him insisting on more. He was angry and so was I.

I checked my email frequently. Two days later a message came informing me that I could pick up my visa three business days subsequent to its receipt, which would be the day I was scheduled to leave. My flight left at 4:00 p.m. so I figured that the account could be opened if I went to the bank immediately after getting the visa.

The day after I arrived I went to the notary's office to make them aware I was in town and was still working diligently to provide the necessary bank account. Doubts as to whether the buyers were still even interested weighed on my mind. The lawyer didn't seem to know where things stood so she organized a meeting for Tuesday afternoon, 24 hours before I was to leave.

At the meeting everyone showed up except Alejandro. I met the buyer and we sat down with the lawyer and Alejandro's partner, Martin. After five full months of putzing around, presumably so everyone could get their documentation in order, it came to light that **not one** party involved had done everything they should have. I was concerned the whole time that it was me who was gumming up the works, but it was me, the real estate agents, the buyers, and their lending banks. Now it was either do or die. The lawyer informed me that the story Alejandro had told me about it being difficult to cancel *Infonavit* financing was as correct as all the other malarky he had told me, patently false. The financing had actually been cancelled but could be reinstated. The buyers were motivated, possibly because they were getting such an unbelievable deal, so we agreed to proceed as planned. The lawyer suggested I get a real down payment, I had been told that the buyers had given $10,000 pesos, but had not seen one bit of the money. The man said he didn't have money for a 10% down payment, and the bank wouldn't advance it, so we left it at a handshake. Too much had already gone wrong for this to fail, if the man said he and his wife were still interested, I had to take them at their word.

As the meeting proceeded the buyer spoke by speaker phone with his wife who was more aware of the banking and loan details. Alejandro eventually showed up 45 minutes after we started. The lawyer, Licenciada Millan, made everyone aware of what was lacking in the transaction and we all agreed to get our part done. I explained what was happening with my visa and bank account and they convinced me that I should go to immigration and see if the visa was ready that day. Although the email I got specified a waiting period of three business days, it was a standard document that they used for all applicants and was not dated itself. Alejandro drove me to immigration when the meeting broke up. He went in with me and we learned that it would take an hour to finalize, but I would get it that day. I sent him on his way.

After what seemed an eternity my card was ready. I was now a Permanent Mexican Resident and I had my green card to show for it. I went straight to Scotiabank to open an account, Alejandro had introduced me to a banker there on my previous visit, so I had a contact there. There were few bankers seeing clients, and too many people waiting, so I reverted to my original plan and went to Banamex. Their number system gave them an air of organization.

Within five minutes of arriving I was attended to by a banker. She seemed quite inexperienced. She had trouble with all the paperwork and it took her more than half an hour to open the account. During the process, I told her that I planned to receive an electronic payment and would want to make an electronic transfer, so I needed the "Swift" number of the bank. Upon completion of the paperwork she took me to the tellers to make my initial deposit. I asked her again for the number and she got it for me. Her inefficiency at this moment would cost me more stress and hundreds of dollars. She did not mention the minor detail that I needed an access code from her in order to do online or phone banking.

It was fortunate that I had gotten the visa Tuesday because if I had picked it up Wednesday and gone straight to the bank, I may not have had time to get the account opened before my afternoon flight out. Opening the account took an inordinate amount of time, nevertheless a crucial element was overlooked by the woman who opened it. When the paperwork was finally completed, I forwarded the details to Licenciada Millan, thus completing my part of the real estate transaction. The one string left untied was the final signature. On my previous visit I had assigned Miguel with power of attorney for this, but since he was not answering my calls after our miscommunication at the airport, I had no idea if he was too angry to help.

The next day I left Acapulco for what will probably be the last time for years, if not forever.

I was told that the transaction would be done in about two weeks. Time passed. More time passed. Occasionally I would send Licenciada Millan a message and she would reply with cryptic answers about the status of the deal, all of which seemed to be saying nothing was happening. Every few weeks I messaged her again.

Finally, 12 full weeks after our last meeting, on Friday, September 9th, Millan contacted me and said that the final signing of documents would take place the following Monday. Although I hadn't heard those exact words before, I had little confidence everything would be done then. I contacted Miguel because he would have to go to the final signing of documents. I had managed to get him back in my good graces after our missed connection at the airport. Monday came and went without the document signing. The lawyer advised me it would happen Wednesday, two days later. We spoke on the phone and she gave me the final, grim numbers. As I had been informed at our meetings earlier in the year, the buyers were getting loans from two different banks. This meant that the money would be deposited into my account in two parts. The first part would be whittled down to only 1/3 of what I would eventually receive. The lawyer said I had to pay some kind of tax, who the fuck really knows what it was, of $80,000.00 MXN, (Could this be the proposed kick back Alejandro had suggested when the initial offer was made?). Plus I had to give the inept real estate agents their cut, 5%, $34,000.00 MXN. Additionally, I was required to pay $3,213.00 MXN for a title transfer fee. But HSBC wanted more. They said I owed them $1,500.00 USD for closing the trust. Plus they had a cockamamie story that my yearly fee had gone up years previously and, not only did I owe them back charges, but also a penalty for paying late.

When Miguel went to the bank Alejandro accompanied him to collect his commission. After getting his 5%, Alejandro claimed I owed him $10,000.00 MXN more for an assortment of dubious alleged expenses he had had while organizing the sale. Miguel managed to slip out of the bank without giving him the extra portion.

Today is September 21st and I have only received the first deposit, not the second, much larger one. The lawyer told me it would take up to eight business days, so far five have transpired. I continue to be on pins and needles about how this will all shake out.

On September 22nd the second deposit arrived, six days after the signing, so the transaction is complete. If HSBC does not come after me for the other money, I sure as hell am not going to give it to them.

There are two funny twists to the final days of this absurd transaction. First of all, since I did not get the access code for online banking when I opened the account, I could not do the wire transfer I had intended, I could only take my money out of ATMs. I thought I'd get it done over the course of a month, because Citibank has a $1,000.00 USD limit. That would be too easy. Banamex has a $6,200.00 MXN daily limit, so I was restricted to a maximum of $300.00 USD at the exchange rate of the time. It would take me over three months to get all my money out, unless I flew to Mexico to do the transfer in person, spending hundreds of dollars more to do so. I was not in a rush, so I began going to Citibank every day for what would be more than 100 days.

The other chink in my plan came as a result of the type of account I opened at Citibank. I had to reach $15,000.00 USD by 30 days from the date I opened the account in order to get a $400.00 USD cash bonus. Not an insignificant chunk of change. However, at the rate of $300.00 USD per day, I was only going to have

$9,000.00 USD by then. I had to juggle some money and not pay my credit card on time in order to reach the required minimum. This is ironic when thinking of my initial move to Mexico and the way I went about getting enough points for my airline ticket. Maybe it's poetic justice.

- Diary entry in italics

As of this writing, none of HSBC's extortion attempts have come to pass. Now I just have to keep withdrawing $300.00 USD per day until the middle of December. Things could be better, but they could also be much worse. The funds that I was supposed to get are sitting in my account.

As the 100 days of withdrawals progress, I realized today that I am being charged 110 pesos for every withdrawal. This is about $5.00 USD, so I am going to lose another $500.00 USD on ATM fees making these damned withdrawals. If I had known for certain that I could get the money out of Mexico by going down there, I might have done so. I don't trust that to happen as it should though, so I will resign myself to spending another $500.00, out of the pittance I am getting for this sale. I paid just under $40,000.00 USD for the condo in August of 2004. Now, 12 years later, I am going to walk away with about $27,000.00 USD. You could say I paid $13,000.00 in rent during the five years I lived there, $217.00 USD per month. This ignores the fact that I invested another $20,000.00 USD in improvements on the property.

It's October 30th, 2016 and I can't believe that I'm adding more to this chapter. The latest twist began about two weeks ago, over 30 days into my daily withdrawals. On October 17th I went to Citibank and was unexpectedly informed that I had reached my withdrawal limit for the day. I had not withdrawn a penny. I was, and continue to be, very concerned that my account has been compromised. I stayed up until midnight that night so I could be at the bank at the moment more funds would potentially be available. I tried the transaction at 11:58 p.m. and it was declined, as was the attempt I made at 12:02 a.m. The next day I called Banamex and cancelled my ATM card. Although I had no online or phone access to my account, for security reasons, I could inform them my card may have been compromised. They said they'd send me a new one to my address on file. That would not work, I don't own the place anymore. The option they gave me was to have it sent to a bank branch. Tomorrow I return to San Diego for the third time this year. I will deplane, pick up a rental car, and head straight to the Banamex branch location I visited twice, earlier this year.

I have trepidations that something has happened to my account or, as one Mexican friend claims, monies received from property sales using Infonavit financing cannot be withdrawn from the country. Curiously, the 30+ withdrawals I have already made almost exactly coincide with the amount of the regular bank loan the buyers used to pay for their purchase. In a little over 24 hours I expect to have this all straightened out and will wire the funds to my Citibank account in the U.S. What a fucking nightmare this has all been. I can only hope my friend is wrong about the funds' availability and also that nothing has happened to the account.

Spy Movie

I left home at 7:35 a.m. Monday, October 31st, 2016, Halloween. I walked to the bus stop five blocks away and caught my limousine, Pace Bus 250. It takes over an hour to get to the airport, but it's reliable and very cheap, $1.75. Arriving at 9:15 at O'Hare, I went straight to the security line with my boarding pass in hand, I had only a carry-on bag. Somehow my gate, number 22, was at the end of the terminal, although chronologically there were eight others after it.

I rented a car from Thrifty again because of previous positive experiences with them in San Diego. All three times I've rented there now I've used a dark blue Yaris which is a very nice car. My GPS said Tijuana was 30 minutes away, however my trip took 20 because I parked before entering Mexico. I left the car at the same lot I had used the other two times I was there. This turned out to be a minor inconvenience. During the interim between my last visit and this one major construction had happened at this border crossing. A beautiful new pedestrian bridge is up which begins near other parking lots and ends at the train stop adjacent to the gates into Mexico.

Entry into Mexico was easier than ever, I just flashed my Mexican Resident card and was waved in. A short walk led to the cheaper taxis. A man I thought was a taxi driver asked where I was going and I told him, he guided me to a taxi with another driver. He told the driver where I was going and I got in. He would charge $5.00, the standard, overpriced fare to the *Plaza Financiera* where Banamex was located. My driver was very strange and spoke in a sort of whimsical manner, almost like everything he said was a joke. He asked me again where I was going. When we got to the corner the bank is located on he drove by and wasted five minutes going around the block. He projected an air of mental deficiency.

When I entered the bank I went to the kiosk where numbers are given depending on what transactions clients intend to do. I told the woman I wanted to do various things, one of which was transfer money to a foreign account. She gave me a form to fill out. The devil is in the details and the devil was right there with me, I had neglected to save my Citibank account number in my phone and I had no wifi access in Mexico. I panicked momentarily then had the presence of mind to go to the mall across the street and find a coffee shop with wifi. I got the account number and went back. After a short wait I was attended to by a man named Ivan who had a desk behind a partition so I didn't have to broadcast my intentions and concerns to everyone seated nearby. The other representatives were beside the teller row, so privacy is minimal with them.

I told Ivan I had come for my ATM card, he checked and found that, blessedly, it had indeed arrived. He got it and I signed for it. Then I told him I wanted access online and via telephone because when I opened the account I was not given the necessary password. I expected him to give it to me now. He explained that this is a service, (actually an account feature, I would say), that is provided at the moment one opens an account, but cannot be offered later without proof of address. More unbelievable absurdity. I had my electric and water receipts, but they were over three months old, so they were worthless. Next I explained that I wanted to transfer the entire account balance to an account in the U.S. and he told me I could not do that either. Now I was getting upset. I was at the bank, in person, and once again could not get my money. He suggested I find someone to lend me their address, (utilities receipts), so I could gain the access I wanted, but knowing not a soul in Tijuana, this could not be achieved, besides, I'd already tried that the last time I was in Tijuana. I even jokingly suggested he loan me his address because we were newfound friends.

I explained all the difficulties I had had withdrawing money in the U.S. and asked him why I had been denied access, to which he had no reply. I asked him how I could be sure this would not happen again with the new card and he had no answer. Moments before leaving, frustrated and dissatisfied, and without my money **again**, something serendipitous happened, Ivan said the magic words. He offhandedly mentioned that, while here, I could withdraw as much cash as I wanted from a teller using my ATM card. The wheels rapidly started turning. He explained that if I took U.S. dollars the bank would give me a dismal rate of exchange, about a full peso more expensive than at a currency exchange. He inferred that my best option would be to take pesos and go across the street to exchange them for dollars. I concluded my discussion with him as he directed me to Teller #1 where he had a co-worker attend to me without taking a number to do my transaction.

I had just over $363,000.00 Mexican Pesos in my account. I wondered how much I should withdraw. I decided to take $80,000.00 MXN, 22% of the balance, and leave $283,000.00. When back in Chicago, I would again withdraw $300.00 USD at a time. Withdrawing part of the funds would save me many days of bank trips, plus ATM withdrawal fees. With trepidation I got the cash, it took about ten minutes at the teller window. I was glad to be carrying a tote bag in which to receive the cash. $80,000.00 pesos comprises a large stack of money. I handed the bag through the glass and he put four bundles of 100 bills each into it. Ivan had told me to go to the ATM outside before I left the bank in order to activate my card, so I asked the teller if that was still necessary, he said it was.

Now I had a huge pile of cash and I was walking on the streets of Tijuana, nerve wracking moments. I waited in the ubiquitous ATM line and took my turn after a half dozen other patrons. I checked my balance and my card was activated.

$80,000 Pesos

Next I had to swap the money for dollars. I walked across the street to the conveniently located currency exchange and asked to change my pile of dough. The girl did not bat an eye. She gave me $4,500.00 USD and I crossed the street and got a taxi to the border. The driver told me there were now two places to cross, but said one was for people with disabilities, so he took me to the one I needed to use. It was an entirely new structure from the one I had used the two times I was there earlier in the year. It was a *long*, (1/5 or 1/4 mile, at least), beautiful bridge that seemed would never end. It starts at ground level and spirals upward to its top height. At the end it spirals downward in the same fashion. When I reached the end I was pleasantly surprised to see at least six customs officers and only a few dozen people in line. The wait was barely more than five minutes. The officer who checked my documents didn't even run my passport through his reader, he just glanced at it and sent me on my way. Would it be possible to return tomorrow for more cash. It certainly seemed so. Time to contemplate my options.

I discovered that the exit of this new point of revision was not very close to where I parked, so I walked over the bridge had driven across earlier and found my car.

It was 4:20 p.m. I told my GPS to direct me to Citibank in San Diego. At 4:50 I arrived there, parked a block away, and ran over before they closed. I gave the teller my massive stack of cash, relieving myself of the worries of walking around San Diego with stacks of hard currency. I drove to my AirBnB house, a different one from the two previous trips, checked-in, decompressed for a few minutes and went out to watch the Chicago Bears on Monday Night Football. Since Rosie O'Grady's is a Chicago themed bar the crowd was enthusiastically cheering our team on to victory against the Minnesota Vikings, arguably the better team. Meanwhile, the Chicago Bulls were slaughtering the Brooklyn Nets on a nearby TV. Things were looking bright. The Cubs had won game five of the World Series the night before, forcing a game six in Cleveland November 1st. I had been fretting about missing game six because my flight was arriving 45 minutes after it began, but as long as I made my flight and avoided hearing people talk about it, I could watch from the start at home with my trusty Tivo.

As I watched the game I contemplated what to do about the money that remained in my Banamex account. I would risk missing my flight if I went again tomorrow, but since customs and immigration had been streamlined so well, this should not be a problem. Ask anyone and they will probably tell you that you can only take up to $10,000.00 USD into or out of the United States. A little research and I found that that was a myth, if you take more than $10K, you merely have to declare it to Customs, if you do not declare it, you are in danger of having it confiscated. I also learned that taking close to $10K is a cause for suspicion, so it's unwise not to declare large amounts of monetary devices, be they cash, bonds, or anything similar.

Ultimately, I decided to go for broke, liquidate my account, declare it, let the chips fall where they may, and be done with it. This would prove to be an experience that I'll remember clearly for the rest of my life.

Tuesday November 1st, I woke up way too early, not used to the two hour time difference, and wired with worry about the upcoming day. My plan was to be at Banamex when they opened, 9:00 a.m. but first I needed to print the declaration document so I'd have it ready upon arrival at Customs. I also needed to print my boarding pass. There was no printer available at the house where I was staying, but I remembered the shop two doors down from the Mexican Consulate where I had used a computer and printed before, so I went there. The proprietor was about to help an aging Mexican couple type up something but she let me go first. The Customs doc was easy, but Spirit online said my reservation had been canceled. Just what I needed. I went outside and called the travel agency that had booked my reservation. They said my flight had been canceled and told me to call Spirit. Spirit said the flight was operating as scheduled, but

I could only check in by printing my boarding pass and if I did not do so, and did not arrive at least two hours before the flight, I was at risk of losing my seat, moreover I would have to pay the $10 check-in fee. The agent gave me a new record locator and I went back inside to try to print my pass. Now the proprietor was in the middle of helping the older couple and I could tell they were doing their *Menaje de Casa*, the list of their belongings they were taking back to Mexico, as I had done in 2007. This could take a while. I waited 15 minutes, they finished, and I took another crack at printing. It did not work. I'd deal with that issue later.

Back at the border I parked in a better lot so I wouldn't have to walk so many blocks after I cleared Customs. I walked over the new bridge and re-entered Mexico through the imposing steel gates a quarter mile away. At the bank I went straight to window number one as I had previously and saw the same guy as the day before, but was told to take a number and wait. There weren't many people so I was seen at another window promptly. The woman who attended to me had strange news. The bank did not have enough cash on hand to cover my withdrawal. Their cash delivery for the day had not arrived. I would have to go to another branch. This was the last thing I wanted to hear, but would ultimately be a fortunate circumstance. She gave me another branch's address in downtown Tijuana and I headed straight there.

This one was quite crowded. When the receptionist offered me a number I told her what had happened at the other branch and asked if they'd have enough cash on hand. She assured me they would so I took a number and took a seat. As I watched the display on the wall showing which number was being handled, I had hope, things were moving quickly. When my number came up I rose and got in line. The girl at the door told me that the display was wrong and I should sit down and wait until I was called. It was well past 10 o'clock now and my flight was leaving at 1:45. When my turn came I got back in line behind four other people. The tellers were behind ceiling-to-counter clear glass panels with a six-inch split down the center. Nothing about the setup was very discreet.

Arriving at the window I gave the guy my bank card, passport and resident alien card and told him I wanted to liquidate the account. He asked me how much I had in it and I confirmed that it was $283,000 pesos and some change. He called over a supervisor and they conferred and sent me to the opposite end of the counter, presumably because of the large amount of my withdrawal. I stood by the other window as the woman meticulously examined my account activity as well as my documents. I was there for ten minutes. I was asked again what I wanted to do and I repeated that I wanted all the cash in my account. After verifying lord knows what, she sent me back to the guy who I had originally spoken to. I thought that being at her end would be to my advantage because it was in a corner and less people would be able to see when I was handed wads of money. Back in the crowded section, with the same guy, he asked me again what I wanted to do and I repeated that I wanted to liquidate the funds in my account. He started the process but needed a supervisor's pass code, so he called for the same guy who had taken me to the other end of the counter to come back and authorize the exchange. The man was busy and we had to wait until he finished another transaction. Ultimately he and another female supervisor had to sign-on before I would be given my cash.

Once again, the teller asked me to sit down and wait. This time I presumed they were gathering the bills needed to complete my transaction. There was nowhere to sit at this point so I stood there looking at him from 10 feet away until he called me back a third time.

I put my tote bag through the window so he could place the bundles into it less conspicuously than giving them to me. He returned the bag to me and gave each packet of money to me one-by-one. There were five stacks of $500 peso notes, each containing 100 bills totaling $50,000.00 pesos per bundle. Next he gave me another bundle of $500 peso notes, containing 50 bills, $25,000.00 pesos. Finally he gave me a stack of $100 pesos notes 83 thick. Additionally there were a few coins. I would be walking out with 633 notes, a healthy stack indeed.

After receiving more cash than I had ever held in my life, with two dozen people behind me capable of seeing what transpired, I walked out of the bank. The day was warm and sunny, but I couldn't help but sense I was in a dangerous situation where my life and liberty were at risk. I had noticed two currency exchanges on the same street within a block of the branch, so I headed toward the one that had the highest exchange rate. I was confused and had gone half a block before I realized it was not where I remembered it, so I crossed the street and went in the opposite direction toward one whose sign was visible to me.

The currency exchanges there were minuscule, open air storefronts, with space for customers averaging about a meter in depth. The first cashier told me she didn't have more than $2,000.00 USD and, furthermore, she would need an ID with my address on it in order to change any amount higher than that because of a new law. I showed her my passport and resident card, but neither was acceptable, it didn't even enter my mind to use my driver's license because the address on it is not in Mexico. I gave her about $36,000.00 pesos and she gave me about $2,000.00.

Next, I crossed the street and found another place with a pretty, young, blonde girl who was more accommodating. I asked if she could exchange $50,000.00 pesos and she said yes, so I asked if $100,000.00 was possible and she said yes. Finally I suggested $150,000.00 and she agreed again, but said she'd need to get more dollars from another branch. She was very helpful and made it clear that she wanted to accommodate me, but because many locals received their pension payments that day, she did not have enough dollars on hand and neither did her other branch. While she waited for her cash delivery I stepped away so she could assist other clients. I left $150,000.00 MXN with her, naively and unwisely, but I had already passed them through to her and the less I waved those wads of cash around, the better. For five minutes or so I perused the inventory of powders and potions the place next door sold. I didn't see any eye of newt, but there were powders for love and sexual stimulation and all kinds of interesting potions.

I was not feeling an adrenaline rush during these tense minutes, I just felt like I was in a movie. I was as focused as I have ever been, while at the same time

I was overwhelmed by the amounts of money I was handling, and the powerful reality that anyone in my vicinity could make my life very difficult if they knew what I was doing. I could see that each cashier was being honest with me from the adding machine receipts they were giving me, coupled with watching as the money was counted by their electric counting machines. I lost track of how many pesos and how many dollars I had almost immediately after I did the first exchange. It was not lost on me that if I had been able to withdraw the money at the first bank branch I had gone to, it could have been a big mess, I had only seen one currency exchange around there and if they hadn't been able, or willing, to help me, I would've been stuck in a taxi with hundreds of thousands of pesos in my bag, going places I had never been before.

The second girl had come up with $8,000.00 USD. I was three quarters done after that exchange. I re-crossed the street to the first place I dealt with, numbers spinning in my head. The woman was finishing up with a man who said he was shortchanged one peso and was angry. He was shouting that she was a crook. Her funds were limited so she suggested I go to another area some blocks away where they had larger currency exchanges and should be able to fulfill my needs at one location, reiterating that I would need an ID with address. Before I would get into a taxi, I had to exhaust my options in the immediate vicinity.

I walked a block down the street and saw more currency exchanges. The third girl I saw said she could only do $900.00 because of the new law, (the number changed depending on who I spoke to). I gave her a bunch of loose $500 peso notes which did not total that much, so I kept pulling more cash out from the stack of $100s until I reached the right amount, I was nervous and worried about drawing attention to my bag of cash.

Everyone I saw, especially the men, seemed suspicious to me. I feared that anyone tracking my movements would know exactly what I was doing and try to take my bag away from me, or worse. I saw one more currency exchange a half block farther down the street. This one was a little bit larger and actually had a glassed in lobby, albeit with doors that remained open. At this location the cashier was a man. He had all the dollars I needed and I finished my work with him, leaving his window with about $3,500.00 USD.

Now I was holding over $15,000.00 USD, although I only had a vague idea what the exact amount was. I looked for a place to use a bathroom so I could count the money in private, but the places I asked, opticians both, said their facilities were out of order. I was insistent with the second lady, explaining that I just needed a place with some privacy, I didn't need a toilet. She reluctantly let me in.

Once inside I felt claustrophobic and paranoid that I could be held there against my will. I was able to organize the bills, but did not count them. As I left she looked surprised that I was finished so quickly. I was racing against time, too. By now it was past 11:00 and I still had to get to the border, walk the long bridge, count the money, declare it, and wait for customs.

I hopped in the first available taxi I saw and got to the bridge without incident. The most dangerous part of my excursion was done. Before mounting the ramp to the U.S. I stopped at the Mexican Immigration Police's makeshift office at the foot of the new structure and asked if there were a bathroom I could use, there was not. I had to forge ahead. I walked and jogged along the bridge as quickly as I could, knowing I had to stop and count the dollars I had received. If I were to be mistaken about the exact amount of money I had with me, I'm sure it would have raised eyebrows at Customs and it may have thrown a giant wrench into my plan. When I reached the descending part of the ramp I stopped and counted the bills. If I had tried to add up the money as I counted I never would have finished in time. I rifled through each pack of bills and wrote the quantity on its band. It took at least five minutes and when I was done it appeared there was less money than there should have been. That was only a misconception, it was all there, $15,487.00 USD. I wrote the final amount on the Customs declaration form and went down the ramp.

The lines this day were even shorter than the day before. I gave the pretty Customs officer my passport and the form and we joked about how shitty my brand new passport is. The bottom edge is too short for the scanners they use to read it. I have to live with that for the next ten years. When she got it processed she accompanied me to the holding area, gave my form and passport to an officer behind the counter and told me to take a seat. She wished me well, the door locking behind her as she left. I was in lockup.

The facility is brand new, clean, and comfortable, but knowing the door was locked and I was at the mercy of the officers was not pleasant. I knew that I was doing everything as I should, though. No one ever looked in my bag or counted the money. When the man finally said I could go, I thanked him, he released the door lock, and I was off. It was 11:53. I now had less than two hours until my flight.

I had a two block walk to my car, much better than the previous day when it was about four times as far. As I pulled out of the lot I remembered that I still had to get gas or I'd be looking at a hefty convenience fee when I returned my rental car. I found a station and filled up.

Traffic started well, best case scenario I'd be arriving at Thrifty to return my car at 12:32. It looked like I'd make it. Then, as so often happens in California, all lanes of traffic came to a complete halt. I was three miles from the airport, but had no idea when I would actually arrive. We creeped along a bit, stopped a bit, and eventually began cruising smoothly again. I was screaming and angry because I was certain I would miss the flight which would mean spending more time and money in San Diego and missing work the next day. I wanted to watch the Cubs game from the comfort of my home, as well.

I got to Thrifty at 12:40, turned in my car, and ran to the airport shuttle. The wait for other passengers was interminable. I arrived at the terminal at 12:55, 50 minutes before takeoff. I ran up to the counter and asked the uncommunicative, unsmiling girl if she could check me in for the Chicago flight. I explained that I'd tried to print my boarding pass but was unsuccessful. In spite of her ambivalence and minimal customer service, she gave me my pass and an excellent seat and I was off to security, confident I'd make my flight. I was overjoyed. I couldn't believe I'd made it. When I got to the gate the flight was not boarding so I even had time to go buy a sandwich before departure.

Early the following day I went to Citibank with 30% of the cash and deposited it, but one $100 bill kept getting rejected. It was dated 1977 and looked quite different than the newer bills. The bank was not open so I went home. I returned an hour later, deposited the rest of the bounty at the ATM and went into the bank to ask about the old bill. The teller looked at it, ran it through some kind of machine, confirmed it was real, and asked if I wanted to exchange it. I got the last C-note and was on my way. *Adios México.* The odyssey has concluded.

A final note: Technically, according to the lawyer at the notary public, I still owe HSBC $1,500.00 USD for closing the trust. I haven't paid it and don't plan to. This string will remain dangling.

Conclusion:

14 years have passed since I dared to uproot myself and go south. I was in my element wrapped in Acapulco's permanent Summer, but now the city I loved is gone. My experiences were unforgettable and I made friendships that will last a lifetime. Big investments by very wealthy people suggest it may ultimately return to being the tourist paradise of decades gone by. I hope its future is as bright as its past. There's a reason why Acapulco was the premier vacation destination and that essence remains, Te Quiero mucho mi querido Acapulco, adiós.

Appendix

Online Report of Fernando's Murder
(English Translation)
Shooting in Acapulco; Five Dead, Five Injured

A truck loaded with heavily armed gunmen attacked a Federal Police patrol vehicle with high-powered weapons, while, simultaneously, gunmen in another truck shot two men traveling in a small car, on the Costera, the main boulevard, in Acapulco, near the Hacienda Maria Eugenia Hotel.

The attack left five people dead, four civilians, including a mother and her 12 year old son, and another man who was in their vehicle. During the confrontation and crossfire, which occurred at 3:30 p.m., five people were also injured, including a girl who sustained bullet wounds to the head and chest, now in serious condition, and two tourists from Mexico City.

According to the official report, police officers were patrolling the area when they became aware of the attack and were immediately attacked themselves, by men with AK-47s.

An hour after the confrontation, police arrested Ernesto Antonio Rocha Reyes, 26, in possession of a large firearm. He said he was linked to "El Güero Huetamo", an operative of drug trafficker Edgar Valdez Villareal, aka "La Barbie".

When police arrived at the point of confrontation, they realized that the men in the trucks were firing upon a small white car with two men aboard. These men lost their lives. The official report states that two high-powered rifles, 16 magazines and some tactical vests were found at the scene.

Federal Police vehicle number 1367, which carried nine officers, managed to repel the attack while it received multiple bullet impacts, but Officer Mario Garcia Rosas was killed a few steps from the vehicle.

At the moment of peak vehicle traffic on the main tourist avenue, five civilians were killed and five were injured. On both sides of the street a total of at least 13 vehicles received bullet impacts, including one that ended up on top of a taxi. The situation caused panic and chaos among Acapulcans, as well as tourists who were walking in the area, many immediately sought shelter in two nearby hotels, Hacienda Eugenia and Playa Suites, as well as in nearby businesses and offices. Some of these establishments also ended up damaged by bullets, two of them had windows and glass doors destroyed.

According to witnesses, and judging from the quantity of bullet casings found on the ground, the confrontation lasted many minutes. More than 50 police of various types arrived, cordoned off the area, and closed both directions of traffic on the Costera from the Plaza Bahia to the traffic circle at the "Diana", one of the most heavily trafficked places in Acapulco.

An hour later Mexican marines arrived and stayed to supervise and look after the entire area. The official report states that three of the dead were identified as Carlos Miranda Delgado, age 12, and his mother Laura Delgado Tullor, 32 years of age, and a taxi driver named José Adaid Cisneros. The injured were Rosalba Luján Darío, 34 years of age, Paula Darío Peña, 55 years of age, both from Mexico City, as well as Denia Solís Baños, 45, and Antonio Reyes, 56 years of age, both from Acapulco.

An unidentified eight year old girl, wearing a school uniform was in critical condition after receiving a bullet in the chest and another in the head. Of the 13 vehicles damaged there were two pickup trucks headed in the direction of "La Diana", one was a blue Aspen, with multiple bullet holes. The other was a silver-grey double-cabin pickup truck with Guerrero state plates in which the bodies of the 9-year old and her mother were found. In fact, theirs was the vehicle that received the most shots, 25 holes were found in the windshield alone.

On the other side of the median, behind a Federal Police patrol vehicle, remained a line of four cars with bullet holes in them, an Aveo, two Chevys and a Pointer. Inside one, two school backpacks could be seen. In the same lane, alongside the bullet riddled patrol car, a line of abandoned cars remained; a wine colored Bora, a Chevy pickup, a grey Platina, a "blue route" taxi, number 2736, a yellow "community" taxi that was hit by a white Camry that entered the median and drove onto the top of the taxi. Also in the line of cars were another community taxi, (*colectivo*), and a Jetta. At 6:00 p.m., three hours after the events unfolded, the area remained cordoned off, surrounded by hundreds of curious onlookers. At that time firefighters arrived and began to wash down the area as there was gasoline on the ground due to damage to vehicles' gas tanks.

Sixth Victim Dies from Wounds Incurred During the Shootout on the Costera

As a result of the bullet wounds received during the confrontation between assassins and federal police, the 9 year old girl who was shot has died today, Thursday, in the private hospital Magallanes. It has come to light that, according to the father of Monserrat Miranda Delgado, it was the officials of the Federal Police that fired on the Explorer Sport, license plate HA-17445, containing the girl, her 12 year old brother and her mother, who both also died. Yesterday the family of the deceased, found in the white Camry, claimed his body. He was identified as Fernando Galeana Mendoza, a lawyer, about whom officials did not want to divulge more information, although they did reveal the fact that his body had 40 bullet wounds in it when the attack ended.

At 10:30 yesterday morning Military Police were informed by hospital employees that the young girl, who had arrived with serious injuries the previous afternoon, had died, and that her body should be picked up. The girl's family insisted that police and investigators claim the body rather than morgue employees. The child was in the back seat of a pickup truck her mother, Laura Delgado, was driving, headed in the direction of the Naval Base. She was in third grade in Colegio Simón Bolívar and lived with her parents on Martín Alonso Street in the Magallanes neighborhood. A few minutes after police and investigators arrived for the body, the girl's father, Daniel Miranda Abarca, and Pedro Miranda Brito, claimed it.

The Conversation

M=me, C=caller, words in parentheses are my thoughts
Approximately 11:00 a.m., Thursday, January 20th, 2011, my condo in El Roble, Acapulco, Guerrero, Mexico
Phone rings, I answer.C: My name is xx xxxx and I'm a Federal Police Officer. We have received a report that a call came from your phone number, 487-6424, reporting suspicious activity in the neighborhood, around your block. We have a recording of the call.

M: I never made any such call.

C: Well, we have evidence that it came from your number. The caller said he saw some white pickup trucks and vans driving around the block repeatedly. We have a recording of the call. The people I work with do not like those who get involved in things they shouldn't. We are very serious people.

M: I didn't make any call. (How could a call have been made from my place? I am the only person living here, no one has used my phone. Could someone have connected to the phone line outside and it showed as a call made from my number?)

C: We have recorded proof you made the call. My bosses don't like people who mess in other people's business. Do you want to show us that you are not working against us, that you will not make similar calls in the future?

M: Okay, but I didn't make any call.

C: My boss needs to know that you are not reporting these activities to the authorities. Are you aware of the xxxxx gang that is active in Acapulco and has been executing people, beheading people, here?

M: Yes (how could I not be?!)

C: You don't want similar problems to happen to you or your family, do you?

M: Of course not. (This guy's saying he's going to kill me, behead me!)

C: We need you to get 25,000 pesos and give it to us so we can return the evidence of your call, the file, to you and know that you are on our side.

M: Okay, but I don't have that much money.

C: How much do you have?

M: About 800 pesos.

C: How long will it take you to get 25,000 pesos?

M: About five days (stalling)

C: We need you to do this immediately. We are watching you, we are on your street. We are on Calle Amates (a block from where I live).

M: I need time to get that money, I don't have it.

C: How much can you get today?

M: Maybe 10,000 pesos

C: You seem like a tranquil person. Are you a peaceful person?

M: Yes, I don't want any problems.

C: Who lives with you? Just your family?

M: Yes (not wanting to give away the fact that I live alone)

C: How many cell phones are in the house, just two, right?

M: I have no cell phone.

C: You have two cell phones in the house.

M: No! I do not have any cell phone.

C: You are not Mexican, correct?

M: Yes

C: You don't want anything to happen to you or your family, right?

M: No

C: You are not a violent, aggressive person, correct?

M: Correct.

C: How long will it take you to get 10,000 pesos?

M: Maybe two hours

C: How are you going to get the money?

M: I have a friend who I can try to borrow it from.

C: Have you borrowed money from him before?

M: No

C: How long will it take you to get it?

M: About two hours (trying to buy time to get my ass to the airport and out of Acapulco)

C: Where can we meet to get the money? Banamex? Soriana?

M: Soriana is fine.

C: Which is better? Soriana or Banamex?

M: Soriana (it's in a very public place, easily accessible to me)

C: I want you to go to Banamex. I want you to take down this number and deposit the money into this account. Do you have somewhere to write it down?

M: Yes, (shaking, scrambling to find a notepad)

C: OK, take this number down.

(He gives me a long number, about 12 or 16 digits)

C: Did you write it down?

M: Yes

C: Read it back to me. Wait, here's the number again.

(Is he illiterate? He can barely read the number correctly, although his speech was perfectly clear and understandable.)

M: (I read back the number)

C: No, let me give you this number.

(He reads me the same number, but adds more digits)

C: I want you to go to Banamex by 1:00 p.m. and get in line, go up to the teller and tell her that you want to make a deposit into your personal savings account number xxx.xxxx.xxx.xxx. Do not tell anyone what is going on or we will kill you and your family. We do not mess around, we have killed many people in this town. We need you to show us that you are sincere and won't bother us again.

M: Okay

C: Repeat what I told you to say, write it down. "I want to make a deposit into my personal savings account, number xxxxxxxxxxxx."

M: (I read back what I had written.)

C: Okay, what will you be wearing?

M: Jeans and a black t-shirt

C: How are you going to go to the bank? Taxi?

M: Yes, taxi. (I lied)

C: We have people on your block. Go to the bank. Make the deposit.

M: Okay

C: Now, do not hang up the phone. Leave the line open while you are gone. Do not tell anyone what is happening or your family will die.

M; Okay.

C: You must make the deposit by 1:00 p.m.

M: Okay (Let me go so I can do what you're asking, asshole!)

C: Do not hang up the phone.

M: Okay

·

Acknowledgements

Thank you to Shawna Williams for her generous assistance with the cover art and final editing. Special thanks to Bruce Gómez for proofreading and editing help, and general support with this project. Many thanks to Miguel Ángel Acevedo Martínez and Jazmin Mendoza Morales for their kind assistance with details in Acapulco during my absence and for their friendship over the years. Thanks to Neftalí Oliver Arellano for his support and friendship. Thanks to all who participated in the events described here.